The Golf Swing
(illustrated)

The Ernest Jones Method

by

DARYN HAMMOND

Reproduction 2012 by **dutchygolf.com**

In the public domain due to copyright expiration
(original date of publication before 1923)

CLASSIC REPRODUCTION

[The view of the golf swing expressed in this book forms the subject of a series of articles contributed by Mr. Daryn Hammond to *Golf Illustrated* of America.]

First Published, April, 29, 1920

Second Impression, July, 30, 1920

Reproduced by dutchygolf.com 2012

This book may have occasional imperfections such as a couple of missing pictures that were part of the original artifact, but we have taken the trouble to make this book readable, by reformatting the content and rescreening for typographical errors and including most of the referenced figures.

The Earnest Jones method is fantastic and we need more instructional manuals on it.

Fig 1. Ernest Jones before the War

CONTENTS

	LIST OF ILLUSTRATIONS	
	FOREWORD	i
1	THE MENTAL PICTURE	1
2	THE GRIP	7
3	THE SWING	21
4	THE ACTION OF THE WRIST	41
5	THE BALANCE OF THE BODY	55
6	STANCE	65
7	OVERSWINGING	73
8	SOCKETING	83
9	SOME OTHER ENORMETIES	97
10	RECAPITULATORY	101
	ABOUT ERNEST JONES	109

LIST OF ILLUSTRATIONS

FIG.

1. Ernest Jones before the War
2. During the War
3. To-day
4. Down-swing. The body has turned on its own initiative
5. The body has followed the lead of the hands
6. The hands have started the club-head moving but the shoulders have not responded
7. How not to grip the shaft
8. Top of up-swing. The extension of the fingers has been overdone. Control has been sacrificed
9. Top of up-swing. The fingers have not been allowed to extend. The "dead hand" position
10. Top of up-swing. The second, third, and fourth fingers have extended, so giving elasticity to the swing
11. The ideal finish of the shot. The second, third, and fourth fingers are extended to the same extent as in Fig. 10
12. How the club is gripped
13. Another view
14. Note position of forefinger and thumb
15. The line of the shaft across the left hand when the hand is opened after gripping the club as in Fig. 16
16. A proper hold of the shaft
17. The ideal grip
18. The ideal grip
19. Wrong position : left wrist bent outward
20. Wrong position : left hand over-turned
21. Correct position
22. Left hand has not forced club-head back
23. Proper action of left hand
24. Quarter shot
25. Half shot
26. Full iron shot
27. Corollary to Fig. 24

28. Corollary to Fig. 25
29. Corollary to Fig. 26
30. Finish of short push shot
31. Finish of socketed approach
32. Perfect finish of short iron shot. Contrast with Figs. 30 and 31, and note how the club-head has been forced through
33. How the blade of the iron should normally come on to the ball
34. Another view of the type of shot shown in Fig. 32
35. Straight position of wrist
36. Movement of the wrist joint
37. Movement of the wrist joint
38. Straight position
39. Other movements of the wrist joint
40. Other movements of the wrist joint
41. Action of right wrist beginning up-swing
42. The right wrist has bent as far as it will go
43. Straight position of right wrist in follow through
44. Left wrist bending in follow through
45. Shows "give" of fingers in any flexible movement
46. Figs. 46 and 47 exemplify again the essential "give" of the fingers
47. Compare with Fig. 46 where the fingers have not "given"
48. An ideally balanced position at the top of the up-swing
49. An ideally balanced position at the finish of the shot
50. The old-fashioned up-swing : exuberent, yet controlled. A slashing and powerful movement
51. Clumsiness and lack of control
52. Good as far as it goes
53. A frequent sight on the links
54. A trifle too careful
55. Compare with Fig. 50
56. The socketing position par excellence
57. An ideal finish
58. The push shot
59. Note the delicacy and freedom of the finish of this iron shot
60. The finish of a firm iron shot
61. Two perfect iron shots. Note the essential similarity of the positions
62. No suspicion of stiffness or rigidity
63. Finis

FOREWORD

"What is wrong with the teaching of golf?" asks a writer in the *Daily Express*.

"That there is something wrong with it," he goes on, "is realized by all people who attempt to play golf, and by all those who watch them doing it.

"Undoubtedly golf is a difficult game, and undoubtedly it attracts a large proportion of devotees whose only qualification for playing it is their devotion. But it is not on these grounds alone that one can explain the pathetic failure of the average golfer's life, or the tragicomedy that is always being enacted by golfing contortionists over the links of the world. One must seek other causes. One must consider, not only the subject and the pupil, but the teacher.

"Broadly speaking, the teachers of golf are either professional golfers or enthusiastic amateurs. In the main, the professional golfer knows how to play golf, but not how to teach it; and in the main the enthusiastic amateur knows neither how to teach it nor how to play it.

"It is one of the characteristics of golf that every exponent of it, no matter how immature his knowledge, no matter how spurious his methods, has moments of exaltation in which he is convinced that he has discovered the true secret of the golf swing, and that he must at once proclaim his discovery to the world at large. Probably what he has discovered is some bad trick which, combined with certain other bad tricks (constituting what he is pleased to call his swing), succeeds in giving him greater length or greater steadiness - for a while. Thereupon he rushes into print. Whereupon some other golfer, whose own box of tricks has gone unutterably to pieces, ingeniously works the new artifice into his golfing system, and emerges temporarily triumphant - not, however, because of the thing which he has taken pains to acquire, but because of the confidence (ill-founded though it may be) with which that thing has for the time being endowed him. And so the process goes on, in an ever-widening circle. Then the original prophet discovers that what he fondly imagined to be illumination is really hallucination; but even now his impulse to kick himself is arrested by some fresh flash of inspiration, obviously,

THE GOLF SWING

unmistakably the real thing this time, and off he goes again. . . . He is a dear, human, lovable fellow, but he is a deadly foe to good golf.

"It is another of the characteristics of golf that the ability to teach it does not necessarily flow from the ability to play it; the champion golfer has probably enunciated at least as much false doctrine as the enthusiastic amateur. It should be borne in mind that the professional golfer has always lived in an atmosphere of golf; to him, indeed, golf is 'second nature' - a matter of instinct. He has a trained hand, but he has not a trained mind. What happens? He is asked to explain how he executes a particular shot; in a word, he is asked to explain how he does a thing which to him is instinctive, a problem which might well harass even the most highly trained mind; and it is not surprising that the professional should flounder. It would, indeed, be surprising if he did not flounder.

"The floundering is naturally worst when he attempts the explanation in writing; for in the first place he has not the art of writing, and in the second place he is unable to help out the explanation by an actual demonstration of the shot. The accidental is mistaken for the essential, the responsive for the initiatory, coexistence for causation, the sign for the thing signified. The results are seen in a bewildering mass of print, both in magazine articles and in book form; and they are reflected in the grotesque performances of countless golfers over the face of the earth. The writer is himself a sufferer, and this is his *cri de coeur*"

* * * * *

The present writer took up golf about ten years ago, when he was thirty. He had not been a cricketer, nor, in fact, had he indulged in any game in which a ball has to be hit, except lawn-tennis; and at lawn-tennis he had achieved but little success, because it was not until he took up golf that he grasped the only two ideas that matter in lawn-tennis: following; the ball on to the racquet and "hitting through." For a few months he played golf "in the light of nature" and derived - and gave to others - considerable enjoyment. It was then borne into him that golf was a game that he was likely to continue to play until old age, or something not less drastic, intervened, and that consequently it would be sane to try to acquire a sound method. He consulted the nearest professional.

FOREWORD

This professional was a good fellow, and he played a fine game. He was animated, however, by an overwhelming passion for analyzing the swing, and it had never occurred to him that his powers of observation and deduction were unequal to the task. Nor did it occur to the writer until he had lived through six months of tribulation, during which he had heroically endeavoured to play golf by turning over the left wrist as far as it would go at the beginning of the swing, by squeezing his right elbow into his side, by tucking his left knee into his right knee, and his right knee into his left knee, and, above all, by straining every nerve to get into a statuesque position somehow or other at the finish of the swing, whether the ball had been toed, heeled, sliced, pulled, or topped.

The writer then took advice from another professional. This excellent fellow was not at all of the analytical turn of mind. He had but few theories, but he enunciated certain propositions which, though they appeared somewhat crude at the time, are now seen to be full of elemental truth. The writer now cordially subscribes to such dicta as, "The golf swing ain't a trick"; "You don't have to wriggle about like an eel: you just stand up to the ball and hit it"; "There's only one thing to remember - you've just got to put the club round your neck both ways"; "Not so much foot-work, sir; golf ain't a sparring match."

On the whole the writer emerged a better man for this cold-douche treatment, and he was given a handicap of 18.

He then began to read every article and book on golf in the English language, and so great was his thirst for knowledge that he deplored that golf had not become part of the literature of Germany and France. He coquetted with many notions and ideas, and one of these, "the straight left arm," stood him in such good stead for a while that his handicap came down to 12. (He now knows why the notion of the straight left arm subsequently played him false.)

This experience was followed by strange lapses from golfing sanity, but the writer was patched up from time to time by various professionals, and his handicap was reduced to 10. He had now got rid of many false ideas with regard to the swing, and had adopted certain useful ideas, with the result that his game showed an all-round improvement, which brought his handicap down, first to 8, and then to 5.

THE GOLF SWING

It is easier, however, to get rid of false ideas than to get rid of bad habits, and the even tenor of his game was liable to be gravely disturbed by recurrences of tricks picked up or accentuated in the early days of his training under the pseudo-scientific professional.

The most persistent and the most demoralizing of these tricks was that common phenomenon of the swing - "body in too soon." In the periods of impotence produced by this scourge, every remedy known to the literature of the game and the Solons of the links was tried; and the writer, discarding one after another, came to place faith in the doctrine enunciated in a small book on golf bearing the engaging title, "The Simplicity of the Golf Swing." In a nutshell, the principle on which that doctrine is based is that at the beginning of both the up-swing and the down-swing it is the shoulders that move first, and that one should, therefore, leave it to the shoulders, in turning, to suggest the proper relative movement to arms and hands. This principle has the merit of extreme simplicity - it presents one concept, one mental picture, instead of a dozen; and in the writer's case it had for a time the effect of facilitating the timing of the full swing. It was not long, however, before first the short game and then the long game went utterly to pieces. The shot became a ponderous, lumbering affair, as unlike the quick, crisp movement of the professional as it was possible to be.

The writer now applied himself to the discovery of some other simple mental picture of the swing. He was convinced that, whether the shoulders moved first or last, good results would not be obtained by consciously trying to move them first. What the golfer has to do is to get into the best hitting position at the top of the up-swing. It may be that in doing this his shoulders will move first. It may be, on the other hand, that if he *tries* to move his shoulders first he will *not* get into that position. The instinct to turn the shoulders may be so strong that the shoulders will do their full part in the swing if the mind ignores them altogether, and concentrates itself on, say, moving the club with the hands. Indeed, after much thought, observation, and trial, the writer came to the conclusion that this was so, and that unless the shoulders were left to look after themselves, their part in the shot was likely to be over-emphasized and the shot impaired.

About this time (July, 1916) it was stated in the newspapers that Ernest Jones, the Chislehurst professional, who had had a leg shot off in France in March, had played round the Royal Norwich links (standing on one leg for each shot) in 83, and a little later, playing with David Ayton, he (still on one

FOREWORD

leg) had holed out the Clacton course - a long course - in 72. It was at once clear to the writer that Ernest Jones at all events must have thoroughly acquired the art of obtaining his results with the minimum exertion, and the writer lost no time in getting once more into touch with a player whose game he had always admired.

Before the war Ernest Jones had been one of the most promising golfers in the metropolitan district, and the Chislehurst Golf Club, the late home of the Empress Eugenie, had come to be known as the home of Ernest Jones.... Though he had not headed the list at any of the most important meetings, Ernest Jones had always been "there or thereabouts." He never failed to qualify for the Open Championship, he generally appeared well toward the top of the final lists, and his scores were uniformly sound. In the *News of the World* competitions he was wont to qualify, and to give a good account of himself in the subsequent rounds; and he did excellent work in the French Championship. In the Kent Championship he adopted the role of runner-up, and in three consecutive finals he lowered the record of three links - Eltham, Hythe, and Herne Bay. There can be no doubt that in the normal course of events Ernest Jones would have attained front rank among his fellow-professionals well before he was thirty. Then came the war....

Jones was ready to respond to the call of King and Country, and in January, 1915, he - along with many other golfers - joined the Army. In November he was out in France, near to Loos; he went through the winter unscathed, but was badly wounded in March, 1916, by rifle grenade. Some sixteen pieces of metal were removed from his head, his right forearm, and his right leg, and this leg was subsequently amputated close below the knee. Nevertheless, the enemy had so far failed to destroy the golfer in him that four months later he was performing the incredible feat of holing out a long and testing course in an average of fours, handing his crutches to the caddy precisely seventy-two times in the round.

The achievement becomes the more startling when it is considered that Jones is a slightly built man on the short side - his height is under five feet six inches and his weight less than 10 stone: he was therefore unable to rely on any reserve of brute force.

His method of hitting the ball had always been conspicuously easy and decisive. In his use of the hands and the fingers he resembled Vardon, but his swing was flatter and rather more compact than Vardon's, and it was accompanied by less suggestion of power, but perhaps even greater suggestion of speed. It was a method which *primâ facie* would stand well the ruthless test that was to be applied to it.

Ernest Jones, moreover, was known to his fellow-professionals, and to some fortunate amateurs, as a golfer who had brought an uncommonly penetrating mind to bear on an uncommonly perplexing subject. He was known as a player of original views, a player who had satisfied himself about the mechanics of the swing, and who played the game fully concious of what he was doing and why he was doing it.

When the writer first saw Jones after his convalescence he had just got his artificial leg, and though obviously embarrassed by it, he played noteworthy golf in an exhibition game with Vardon, Taylor, and Braid. One saw that he experienced difficulty in finishing the shot freely - the right leg came lumbering forward after the ball had been hit - but there was the same clean, crisp hitting as before. At the time of writing, however, he is on better terms with the artificial leg, and though it still complicates the question of balance, especially when the stance is uneven - as it frequently is at Chislehurst - it does not succeed in helping Jones's opponents to anything like the extent they would naturally expect it to do. Sequences of fours interrupted by threes continue to be the order of Jones's day.

The writer found that Jones was convinced that the golf swing could be readily taught and consistently performed only if it were conceived as one movement, that various members of the body (including the shoulders) were normally anxious to get busy too strenuously and too soon, and that the only way of insuring their working in due co-ordination with the other members of the body, notably the hands and the fingers, was to treat them as disastrous leaders, but as wholly admirable followers. The basis of the swing, as Jones had worked it out before the war, was the proper action of the hands and fingers.

His accident had put his theory of golf to the touch, and had intensified his faith in it; and it was not long before the present writer was swinging a golf club with a decisiveness which had previously seemed beyond his range of accomplishment.

More than ever Ernest Jones felt the artist's itch for asserting his point of view before the largest possible audience; but though at the very forefront of

FOREWORD

vivâ voce teachers, he was not a practised writer; nor would he resort to the device of commissioning a golfing journalist to produce a book purporting to be written by himself. It was in these circumstances that the present writer came to essay the task of explaining the principle and the method which Ernest Jones had made so vividly clear to him on the links.

The writer is fully aware of the danger of conveying impressions other than those intended to be conveyed, and he earnestly asks the reader to check the impressions formed by him by immediately trying them out on the links with club and ball.

In this book one lesson only is taught, and that one lesson is taught all the time. Each chapter is but a re-statement - from a different angle - of the principle enunciated in every other chapter. The risk of wearying the reader by reiteration has been preferred to the risk of leaving him in doubt.

"Surely," says the writer in the *Daily Express*, "among the thousands of golfers in the two hemispheres there is some one person who can make this plague of a game intelligible?"

There is. He is Ernest Jones. And if there is anything unintelligible in the following pages, it is the writer, and not Ernest Jones, who is at fault.

THE GOLF SWING

FOREWORD

Fig 2. During the War

Fig 3. Today

1 THE MENTAL PICTURE

It will have been gathered from the preceding chapter that in this exposition of the golf swing the writer's aim is not to decide such points as whether in the up-swing the shoulders move before, at the same time as, or later than, the hands, but to suggest to the reader that mental picture of the physical processes involved which will help him to obtain the result he seeks.

In the long game the golfer wants the utmost length that he can get without sacrificing control. It is of little use to him to hit a ball "to blazes"; for almost invariably it is difficult to get back from that locality to the green. It will not even serve his purpose to hit one long straight ball at every second shot. Obviously what he requires most of all, if he is sane, is control. In the short game indeed, control is everything. Nothing else matters.

The primary question, then, for the golfer is how to control the behaviour of the ball - that is, how to gain control over the club head.

Control over the club head connotes two things - power and "touch/' Power can be gained by gripping the club in the palms of the hands, but it is given only to few people to obtain "touch" in that way. "Touch" can be obtained by gripping the club lightly in the fingers, but power cannot be gained in that way. Something between the two methods of gripping is required.

THE GOLF SWING

There are, perhaps, two natural methods of holding any implement with which one intends to strike. If one were about to break stones or fell a tree, one would instinctively take hold of the hammer or the hatchet deep in the palm of the hand. The grip would adapt itself to the notion of power. If, on the other hand, one were nonchalantly decapitating daisy-heads in the course of a country walk, one would instinctively hold one's cane lightly in the fingers: the grip would adapt itself to the notion of flexibility and speed.

The golf ball is a light thing compared with the stone, a heavy thing compared with the daisy-head; and the golf club is a light thing compared with the stone-breaker's hammer, a heavy thing compared with a cane.

Jointly, then, the golf club and golf ball should suggest to the mind a compromise between power and speed, between "hefti-ness" and flexibility.

It is the blending of these two qualities which baffles the average golfer. He is apt to attach by far too much importance to power, and the result is that he manipulates his club ponderously and ineffectively, never for one moment realizing the idea of speed or "touch/ and usually failing to achieve his one objective - power. His mental picture is ill-conceived, and therefore his action goes astray. His hands and fingers have failed to do their full share of the work, and consequently his body comes into the shot at the wrong time and in the wrong positions.

In the revolutions of a wheel the speed of the hub bears a fixed ratio to the speed of the rim, but the golfer who mistimes his shot suggests the analogy of a wheel in which the hub and the rim are at variance, the hub being determined to increase the ratio of its speed to the speed of the rim. The result, in the example of the wheel, would be broken spokes and a buckled rim. In the case of the golfer, the arms are too flexible to break (though the club is not), but the result is a jerky and retarded, not a quickened, movement of the club-head; moreover, the course of the club-head is out of truth: the shot is a failure.

The fingers bear to the other members of the body involved in the golf swing a somewhat similar relationship to that which subsists between the toes and the other members of the body involved in walking. If one walks, thinking only of the action of the hips, one will instinctively take long strides, and the gait will suggest considerable power but little "life." If in walking one thinks only of the action of the knees, the effect produced will be one of

1 THE MENTAL PICTURE

feebleness and ineffectiveness. If, however, one walks concentrating on the action of the toes and the ankles, the stride will be short and quick, and great flexibility and vitality will be felt and suggested. The reader is invited to make the experiment and enjoy the sensation of the toes gripping the ground and promoting a rapid forward movement of the legs. The type of gait, it will be observed, is the outcome of the mental picture.

It is so with golf. The swing is the outcome of the mental picture. Let the reader visualize clearly a swing in which the motive force is applied by and through the hands and particularly the fingers; let him cease to care what other physical processes are involved; and let him rest assured that if his brain prompts the hands and fingers to do their work, the other members of the body will probably do theirs. If he does this, he will be well on the way to achieving that crisp, decisive method of hitting a golf ball which makes the professional's game the despair of the ordinary amateur player.

The golfer should fix it firmly in his mind that his object is not to pit his strength against the inertia of the golf ball, but to lash a responsive ball away by flinging the club-head at it at the highest possible speed. Speed is the *sine qua non*.

Much learning has been devoted to the question whether the golfer's action is a swing or a hit. Most good golfers say it is a swing, but what most good golfers have in mind when they make a shot is to hit. This kind of bewildering inconsistency is rampant in golf. The mental picture suggested by the idea of sweeping the ball away may be instinct with rhythm, but it does not suggest that dash, that speed, that crispness, that "pinch," that "nip," which is of the essence of the modern professional's action.

The golfer should picture to himself that he has to hit the ball away with the club-head, and that in order to do this most effectively he must set the club-head moving and keep it moving all the time by hand and finger work. He must not give a moment's thought to the action of the legs, or the feet, or the hips, or the shoulders, or even to keeping his eye on the ball. He must be preoccupied, he must be obsessed, by the one idea of bringing the clubhead on to the ball by means of a persistent movement of the hands and fingers. He must not think of keeping his left arm and the club-shaft in one line as long as possible (this idea shows a complete lack of appreciation of the functions of hands and fingers); he must not think of keeping his left arm stiff (this, in so far as it happens, is an effect, not a cause); he must think of nothing other than the one idea of making the club-head move all the time with the hands and fingers, and of letting arms, shoulders, hips, legs, and feet respond unhampered to the call made upon them. As a fact, if he goes on taking the club back by finger pressure as far as it will go, he will find that his left knee will automatically turn toward his right, that the left side of his left foot and the left heel will slightly leave the ground, that the left shoulder will turn underneath the chin, that the left arm will be moderately extended (certainly not fully extended or rigid), that at the top of the swing the hands and wrists will be underneath the shaft of the club, that the sole of the club-head will be facing upward, and so on. If any of these effects are not produced, it will not help him consciously to insert them into the up-swing. He must get back to the basic notion of persistent finger work, and he will find that in so far as the traditional symptoms are not exhibited in his swing, he has failed somewhere in that finger work. Somewhere in the upswing the finger work has been relaxed and has failed to give the necessary impetus to the other, the subordinate processes. Similarly, if the down-swing betrays any lack of rhythm, if the body moves too soon or too late or in the wrong curve, if the weight does not follow the club-head - if, in short, anything goes wrong with the swing, let the player try to discover where he has failed in his hand and finger action. He is almost sure to find that at some point or other the finger action has ceased to assert itself, so allowing processes which should be subsidiary and accommodating processes, to take the initiative. If the mind is concentrated on manipulating the club-head by means of hand and finger work, the body can hardly get into the shot too soon, and if the player is determined to let everything respond which wants to respond to the impulse suggested by the hands and fingers, the body is not likely to lag behind. The hands and fingers must so control the club-head that at the vital moment they are ready to make the club-head (which up to that point in the down-swing has been behind the hands) lash through the ball, pulling hands, arms, shoulders, and legs after it.

If one considers for a moment the movements which take place in an ordinary Indian club exercise, one will realize that the performer's mind is concentrated on the work of the hands and fingers. The arms, the shoulders, the body, the legs and the feet respond sympathetically to the movements suggested and set up by the work of the hands and fingers. They do not initiate, but on the other hand, they do not retard. Their province is to be ready and willing to move in order to allow the manipulation of the clubs to proceed with the utmost freedom, precision, and rhythm. It may be that the shoulders and other members of the body do in fact move at the same time as

1 THE MENTAL PICTURE

the hands, but the essential thing for the mind to dwell upon is not what movements take place, but how and where to apply power. For if power is properly applied the accessory or accommodating movements are not likely to give trouble.

THE GOLF SWING

Fig 4. Down swing.
The body has turned
on its own initiative

Fig 5. The body
has followed the
lead of the hands

Fig 6. The hands have started the
club-head moving, but the
shoulders have not responded

THE GOLF SWING

2 THE GRIP

The view that the execution of the golf swing depends on hand and finger action brings out emphatically the immense importance of the grip. The grip is seen to be at the root of the matter; for clearly the player's control over the club depends primarily upon it. His hold of the shaft must be firm yet it must be flexible. Here are two qualities which appear to be incompatible with each other, and it is the golfer's first duty to acquire that method of gripping the club which will allow him to bring these apparently incompatible qualities together in sweet accord.

The old-fashioned palm grip gave power, but not flexibility or "touch."[*] The double V grip gives both power and touch, but not unity of action to the two hands. The interlocking grip conduces to that unity of action, but only at the expense of both power and touch (for it puts the powerful forefinger of the left hand almost out of action). The overlapping grip, however, has all the qualities and none of the defects of the other varieties. Its superiority might, indeed, be inferred from the fact that it is the grip of almost every professional golfer and of nine first-class amateurs out of ten.

It is unfortunately the fact, however, that the majority of golfers who use an overlapping grip entirely miss one of the essential features of this form of grip. They realize that the little finger of the right hand is to be allowed to ride

---

[*] The writer speaks always of the normal case, and takes no account of what long practice or genius may accomplish with any method under the sun.

2 THE GRIP

over the forefinger of the left hand, so that the hands may have some chance of acting as one, and they realize that the overlapping grip is a finger grip. What they do not realize is that the very essence of the grip is the dominating part played by the forefinger and thumb of each hand.

The advice usually given - though never practised by the expert - is that the first step in gripping the club is to lay the shaft along (that is, parallel with the joints of) the fingers of the left hand. The position indicated is shown in Fig. 7 and the consequent positions of the hands at the top of the up-swing are as shown in Figs. 8 and 9. The position in Fig. 8 is unusual, because the player instinctively realizes that such a position would give him no control of the club, and allows the shaft to move into the palm of his hand as the up-swing proceeds. The result is that that which set out to be a finger grip becomes a palm grip, a grip lacking in flexibility and the capacity to produce high speed in the club-head.

The true finger grip is to be achieved, not by laying the club along the fingers of the hand, but by the following method:

1. Lay the face of the club-head against the ball, allowing the club to take its natural lie.

2. Take hold of the shaft with the thumb and forefinger of the left hand, pressing them together (Figs. 12 and 13). Note that the V made by them on the top of the shaft is a short one, the crook of the forefinger being pronounced and slightly lower than the tip of the thumb.

3. Wrap the other fingers round the shaft (Figs. 14 and 16).

Note. -

(a) The back of the hand is not on the top of the shaft, but at the side of it - that is, facing toward the hole. As the player looks down, he should see the knuckles of the first and second fingers, but not more than a suggestion of the knuckle of the third finger. If the back of the hand is further on the top of the shaft, the wrist and forearm will be stiffened, and the swing will consequently be cramped. If the back of the hand is further to the side (that is, more toward the hole), then the left wrist will tend at the beginning of the up-swing to bend outward (a movement known to anatomy as the "extension of the wrist-joint," and utterly out of place in the golf swing: Fig. 20). If, however, the club is gripped as shown in Figs, 17 and 18, and the proper mental picture of the processes involved in the up-swing has been conceived, the fingers in initiating the movement of the club-head will automatically bring the wrist and forearm into the ideal position. There will be no "extension of the wrist-joint," and the hand and forearm will turn as shown in Fig. 21.

(b) Though the back of the hand is not on the top of the shaft, or facing the sky, the V between the thumb and forefinger *is* on the top of the shaft. It will probably require some little practice in order to get the V into this position without bringing the back of the hand too far over the shaft.

(c) The grip is dominated by the pressure of the forefinger and thumb, the second, third, and fourth fingers contributing in decreasing order to the control of the club so obtained.

(d) If the fingers and thumb are opened out, the shaft will be found to lie, not along the finger joints (Fig. 7), but along a line from the tip of the forefinger, across the lower part of the second finger, the root of the third finger, and the cushion of the palm (known in palmistry as the Mount of the Moon). See Fig. 15.

4. Having mastered the grip of the left hand, place the right hand about the shaft so that the little finger rides easily over the forefinger of the left hand, and the thumb and forefinger grip the shaft in similar formation to that of the thumb and forefinger of the left hand. The knuckles of the first and second fingers are visible to the player, the V between the thumb and forefinger is on the top, or almost on the top of the shaft, and the grip is secured mainly between the crook of the forefinger and the thumb, though the second, third, and fourth fingers, in descending order, play their part.

To sum up, the grip (Figs. 17 and 18) is dominated by the forefingers and thumbs of both hands, the other fingers fulfilling a necessary but ancillary function.

The reader will be able to satisfy himself by experiment, without a club, that if he closes all the fingers of his hand as tightly as possible, he will stiffen the wrist and forearm and even the upper arm, whereas if he grips as firmly as possible with the forefinger and thumb he can retain a completely free wrist, forearm, and upper arm. Such freedom of action, coupled with control of the

2 THE GRIP

club, means the playing of good golf, whereas a conscious tension at any point in the mechanism other than the grip of forefinger and thumb is an obstacle to good golf. It is on these grounds that so much importance is attached to the question of gripping the club.

Figs, 10 and 11 indicate the respective positions of the hands and fingers at the top of the up-swing and at the end of the follow-through. They show that the grip is preeminently a finger grip, and they make clear the nature of the work done by the second, third, and fourth fingers. From this point of view Fig. 10 should be compared with Figs. 8 and 9.

THE GOLF SWING

Fig 12. How the club is gripped

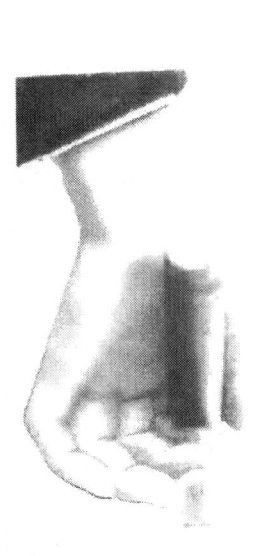

Fig 13. Another view

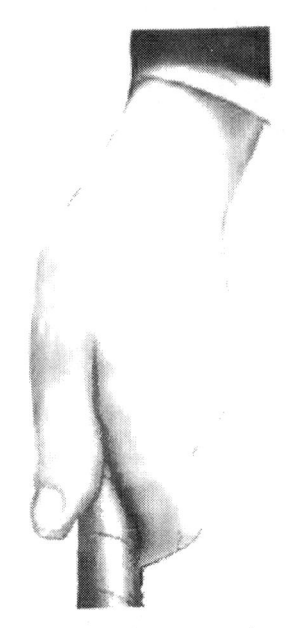

Fig 14. Note position of forefinger and thumb

2 THE GRIP

Fig 11. The ideal finish of the shot. The second, third and fourth fingers are extended to the same extent as in fig. 1

THE GOLF SWING

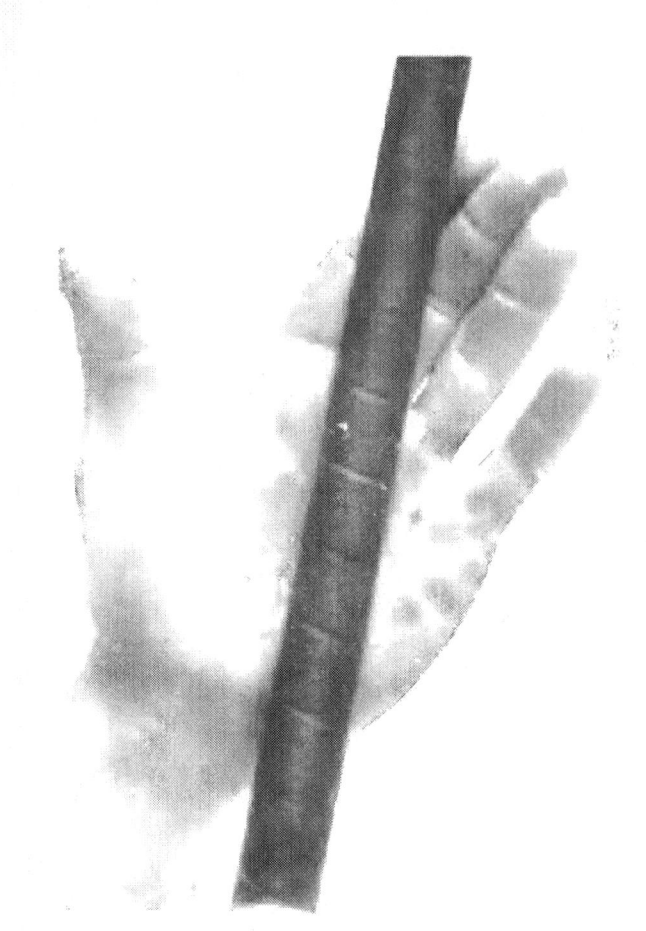

Fig 15. The line of the shaft across the left hand when the hand is opened after gripping the club as in fig 16

2 THE GRIP

Fig 16. A proper hold of the shaft

THE GOLF SWING

Fig 17. The ideal grip

2 THE GRIP

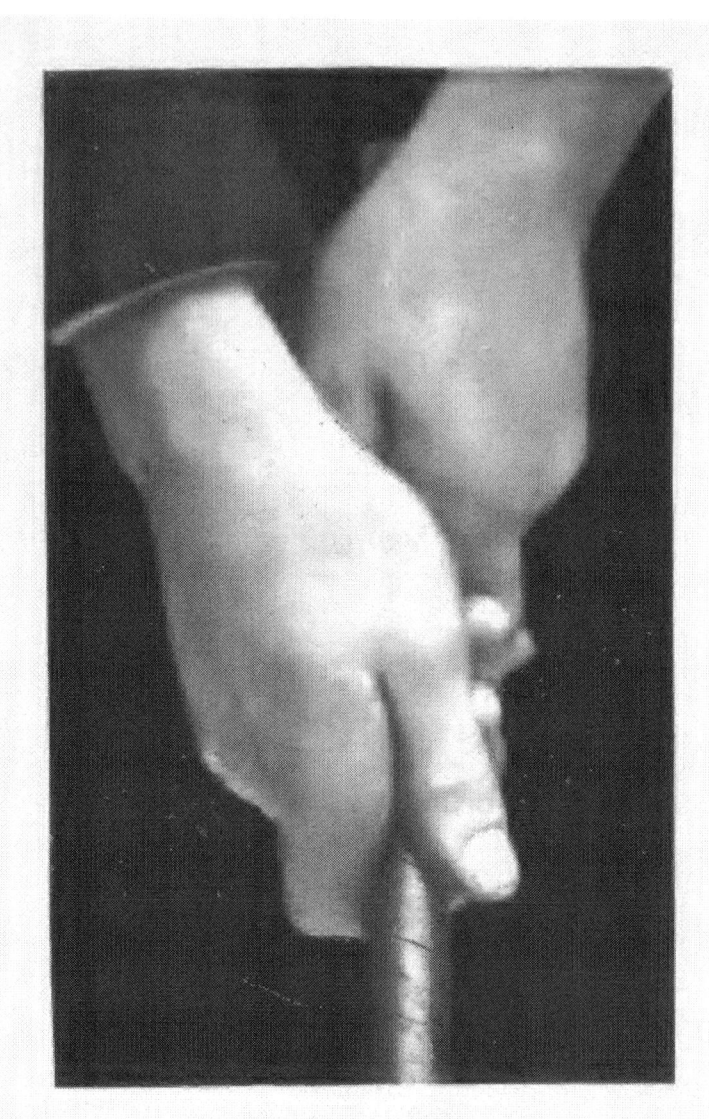

Fig 18. The ideal grip

THE GOLF SWING

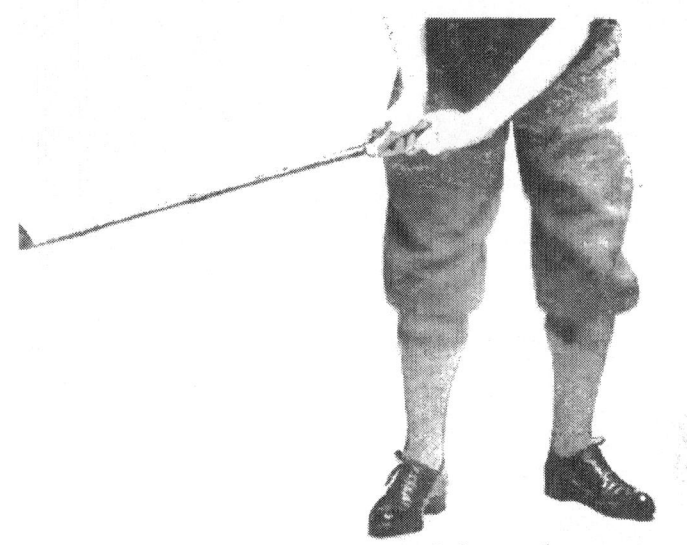

Fig 19. Wrong position - left wrist bent outward

Fig 20. Wrong position - left hand over-turned

2 THE GRIP

Fig 21. Correct position

THE GOLF SWING

Fig 22. Left hand has not forced club-head back

Fig 23. Proper action of left hand

2 THE GRIP

3 THE SWING

THE WAGGLE.

Having satisfied himself that he knows exactly how the club should be gripped, the player should practise the movement, preliminary to the swing, inelegantly described as the "waggle." Much is to be gained from the waggle treated as an exercise. The waggle should be performed, not aimlessly, but by the conscious application of power by the ringers. The golfer should move the club-head backward, and then move it forward, thinking only of producing the movement by finger work. He will soon become at ease with his grip and on good terms with his club; he will get the "feel" of the club, and become conscious of an increasing command over its movements. In doing this exercise he must determine -

(1) to grip the club firmly in the forefingers and thumbs.

(2) to keep every other part of the body relaxed, notably the wrists, arms, and shoulders.

(3) to apply the motive power continuously, persistently, by the fingers.

If these three points are observed, then:

(a) the body can never lead; and

3 THE SWING

(b) the body will always follow.

The player will quickly become an expert waggler, and he can then extend the waggle until it becomes a complete backward and forward swing. If the same principles be always borne in mind, the shoulders will turn and the knees will bend in due time and place.

This backward and forward swinging (which incidentally is an excellent physical drill) rapidly promotes that sense of balance and that feeling of control over the club which hundreds of rounds of golf often fail to give; and no matter how expert the golfer may be, no matter how much he may be "on his game," he cannot fail to derive advantage from the exercise, provided that it is performed, never perfunctorily or carelessly, but always with the resolve that the three fundamental principles of grip, relaxation, and finger work shall be consciously and conscientiously carried out. The exercise so practised will produce not only freedom and certainty of movement, but that habit of mental concentration which golf demands as much as anything else in life, whether work or play.

If the body and mind are constantly trained in this manner, the actual hitting of the ball is not likely to present any grave difficulty. Naturally, the very presence of the ball will tempt the golfer to forget one or more of the three articles of faith, and he will often fall before the temptation; but so long as he realizes that the failure of the shot must be due to the failure to observe one or more of the three articles of faith, and to nothing else, and is to be cured by due observation of those articles and by nothing else, his progress in the game will not be long delayed.

The Quarter-Swing

It is best to begin by making quite short shots with an iron club - a mid-iron or a mashie: what is known as a quarter-swing or a half-swing (Figs. 24, 25, 27, and 28). It is this movement which forms the essential part of the full swing, and it is because this movement is so often absent from the full swing that the ball is not really hit away, but is merely pushed away by the club (Fig. 30). When this relatively slow and powerless movement is performed, the fingers and hands have failed to dominate the movement as the hands come toward their lowest point in the down-swing. Instead of forcing the club-head from its position behind them to a position in front of them in order that the ball may be hit away in the most definite manner, the hands and fingers have

THE GOLF SWING

failed to exert themselves at the vital moment; they have exercised no leverage over the club, and the shaft and arms have moved through the lower sector of the swing practically in a straight line. In other words, the action of the hands and fingers, obviously essential in the quarter-swing or half-swing, has been absent, and the hands have performed no function other than that of a strap fastening the club to the arms. The control, the power, and the "touch," which should have been in the hands and fingers, have been lost. The shot at the best can only be second-rate. At the worst . . .

It is the omission from the full swing of the fundamental action in the short swing that causes the normal driving of the amateur to lack that unmistakable quality of definiteness which distinguishes professional play. The full swing is therefore to be conceived as an enlarged quarter-swing - enlarged solely in order that greater impetus may be imparted to the club-head.

Slow-Back

The principle of slow-back which is dinned into the ears of every beginner is practised by no first-class golfer. The beginner is led to believe that some subtle magic resides in the process, and he performs the laborious operation as though he were anxious to get the club over his right shoulder without any profane onlooker seeing or hearing what he has accomplished. He is like a thief in the night, or a housemaid circumventing a meat-fly. It is, of course, possible to hit a good shot after treating a golf club in this ridiculous manner. It may be less difficult to hit a good shot in that manner than after snatching the club-head away from the ball as though the golfer had suddenly gone mad or suddenly imagined that the club-head was burning the new half-crown ball away. But the up-swing is neither a funeral rite nor a music-hall trick. It should be just a light, easy, free, flexible movement, pleasing to execute, pleasing to observe. The slow-back doctrine is a clumsy statement of the principle of control. The golfer must obtain and retain control of the club. It is seen that he almost necessarily loses control when he jerks the club away from the ball, and instead of the root principle of control being intelligently explained to him, he is told without ceasing to go "slow-back." He begins to regard "slow-back" as an end in itself instead of a bad means to that end, and he plods on, for ever missing the whole significance of the golf swing.

It may be objected that the person who makes the up-swing at a snail's pace does in fact possess control of the club. This, however, is untrue. In the

3 THE SWING

first place, the movement he makes is not an up-swing at all - it is merely an upward movement, or rather a series of upward movements. There is no swing in it, and it cannot conduce to the development of swing in the downward movement. The phrase "control of the club" means control of the club *qua* golf club, not *qua* sledge-hammer; it connotes the ability to set up speed in the club-head, from the utmost speed that it may be capable of achieving, as in the drive, down to the lowest speed at which it can be induced to move effectively, as in the short putt Such control is not to be obtained by the observance of any shibboleth, least of all the shibboleth of slow-back. The up-swing must be a *swing*, and its only function is that of the best possible pre liminary to the down-swing. It is not an end in itself: it is only a means to an end. It is not a means to that end unless it is light, easy, free, flexible. If it has those qualities, and is controlled, its speed is a matter of no importance. The best golfer is the golfer who has greatest control of the club, and it may well be that he is the golfer who has the quickest up-swing - this being an effect, not, of course, a cause, of supreme control. The beginner should therefore always keep in mind the great question of control, and he must steadily refuse to be side-tracked, whether he is considering, or practising, either the up-swing or the down-swing. As a matter of fact, he would do well never at all to think of the swing in separate parts. The waggle, the up-swing, the down-swing, the follow-through, and all the rest of it, are in reality one thing - the movement by which the golfer obtains, and expresses, his mastery over the club-head. This mastery is to be achieved by the cultivation of proper hand and finger action, by relying on the hands and fingers to provide the initiating motive power - in other words, by setting the machinery going at the fingers.

The Down-Swing

One of the most vital moments in the golf swing occurs just before the up-swing is completed. Even the player who has begun to realize the importance of persistently moving the club-head with the hands, is tempted at this point to forget to carry this action out and to let the body go on twisting on its own account. When this tendency is yielded to, it becomes extremely difficult to give the proper start to the club-head at the beginning of the down-swing; for if the hands fail at any moment they are all the more likely to fail at the next moment. And the right shoulder, instead of being pulled round as a result of an impetus set up and kept up by the hands, will turn on its own account (Fig. 4). Consequently, when the club-head strikes the ball, the shoulders will not be in anything like the position they occupied when the ball

THE GOLF SWING

was addressed, but will be turned toward the hole - they will, in fact, be already more or less in the position they should take at the finish of the shot. This is the normal case of "body in too soon." The player will be told by his caddy that he has cut across the ball or pulled his arms in, and he will be urged to throw his arms out after hitting the ball. Such advice is on a par with the recommendation to lock the door after the horse has gone. The player has not pulled his arms in. His body has turned prematurely and on its own impulse. The arms cannot help coming across the line of intended flight as the ball is struck, and nothing that the player can do as he strikes the ball, or after he has struck it, can be of the least avail. One must get back to the source of the trouble - that point in the swing, possibly in the up-swing, possibly at the beginning of the down-swing, at which the hands and fingers have failed to do their work. (Compare Figs. 22 and 23.)

In most of the books on golf, that vital moment in the swing, the beginning of the down-swing, is passed by in silence, but in one or two of the books greater or less attention is devoted to it. In the Harry Vardon book it is dealt with at some length, and the player is recommended to aim, at the beginning of the down-swing, at an imaginary person behind him. This kind of teaching may conceivably do some good, but it is, in principle, unsound. It does not go to the root of the matter. If in the true swing the club-head passes through certain points, it does not follow that the true swing can be produced by guiding the club-head through those points. In the true swing, the fingers, hands, arms, etc., perform coordinate movements, and if those movements are properly produced, the club-head cannot help following the proper path. To guide the club-head along that path in the hope that the anatomical movements will be sound is to put the cart before the horse, effect before cause. One must begin at the beginning and endeavour to secure the effect desired by mastering the processes of which that effect is the inevitable outcome.

In "Golf Faults Illustrated," Taylor, in speaking of the down-swing, admonishes the reader not to "put on leverage too soon." The meaning here is not too clear, but it may be the same as that conveyed by that golfing commonplace "Don't hit from the top." If it is, then it is diametrically opposed to the injunction of Braid in "Advanced Golf," who directs the player to hit from the top as hard as he can, Taylor is apparently anxious that the player should not force the shot with his body; Braid is apparently anxious that he should take the risk. And so long as the player always applies his

3 THE SWING

power with his hands, letting everything else freely respond to the action so initiated, there can be no doubt that he who hits most vigorously will hit best.

In several other books it is stated that the down-swing is begun by a pull of the left arm. This, at best, is a half-truth, and is misleading. The initiation of the movement is in the hands, and the pull of the left arm is a responsive - an immediately responsive - movement. The operation is simply the operation of hitting - it is instinctive when once the principles of the movement have been mastered; and it is significant that no good golfer who is on his game has ever anything in mind when making a shot other than hitting the ball. He is not trying to hit an imaginary person behind him; he is not trying not to put on leverage too soon, or not to hit from the top; he is not trying to initiate the downswing with a pull of the left arm - he is merely moving the club-head - hitting the ball.

Head-Lifting

Even the resolution to glue the eyes to the ball is an irrelevance. If the player has the hitting idea immovably in his mind, he is sure to look at the ball; the player only fails to look at the ball when that one dominating idea is momentarily absent. If the mind for one instant leaves that idea and concerns itself with anything else, as, for example, the result of the shot, the head will, as likely as not, go up. Moreover, if the mind flits for one moment from the one idea of hitting the ball, the rhythm of the movement will be disturbed, the swing will probably go wrong, and the player's head will inevitably go up - it will be jerked up. Every indifferent player is a victim from time to time to fits of head-lifting. All sorts of "tips" have been devised for the treatment of this malady, but it is common experience that no matter what specific is applied the head-lifting continues. It is, indeed, not to be cured by nostrums, not even by a fixed determination to keep the head down. For head-lifting is usually an effect of a bad swing, not a cause of one. The only real cure for head-lifting or any other golfing malady lies in concentrating the mind on forcing the club-head into action by proper hand and finger work.

Letting The Club-Head Do It

The idea so often put forward of letting the club do the work is misconceived and misleading. The club-head will certainly not do the work if the golfer is anything like so passive towards it. The golfer must learn to make the club-head do the work.

THE GOLF SWING

The illustration of the beginning of the upswing (Fig. 23) bears directly upon this principle. This is a posed as distinguished from an action photograph, and it undoubtedly differs to some extent from what would be revealed by an action photograph. The latter would show a fuller development of the accessory or accommodating movements. At the same time, if the golfer tried to make his movements correspond with those indicated by an action photograph, he would be tempted to give undue attention to the accommodating movements. The posed photograph emphasizes the importance of hand and finger work at the very outset of the swing, and if this idea is allowed to dominate the mind of the golfer (coupled always with the complementary idea of *not interfering* with the full and free development of the accessory or accommodating movements of the other members of the body) the golfer will often achieve something closely akin to golf.

Approach Shots

The significance of the clear mental picture is perhaps most apparent in the approach shot. Where the exact length of the shot can be measured, and where the character of the shot is determined by the hazards and other features of the course, every golfer who has obtained some command over his clubs addresses his ball with confidence. His environment forces the correct mental picture upon him. He cannot escape from it. There is no doubt, no vagueness as to what is required. But in the opposed type of shot, as, for example, an open approach to an unprotected green, with nothing to indicate clearly the length of shot which is called for, the golfer has himself to make up his mind as to the type of shot to be played. Probably half a dozen shots are open to him, and he has to select one of them. He may find difficulty in deciding which is the best, and he may change his mind whilst executing the shot. A large percentage of foozled approaches are due to this cause, as every golfer knows only too well. It is obviously of first importance that the player should never proceed to execute any shot, no matter how short or how easy it may appear, until he has definitely outlined in his mind the type of shot he intends to produce.

The Run-Up

In order to produce this shot the golfer is usually instructed to turn over the right hand on, or immediately after, hitting the ball. If, however, the

3 THE SWING

player concentrates on this turning over of the right hand as a thing in itself, he is not likely to obtain good results. He will probably turn the hand over too soon, too late, or too much, and his action will probably be stiff and artificial. The proper shot can be consistently produced only when the shot is made from the proper point of view; and in the run-up, as in every other shot, the player must get down to the essence of the matter. What is the essence of the run-up? What are the characteristics that leap to the eye when the shot is played by an expert? First, consider the flight of the ball. The ball rises but little from the turf, and the inference is that it has been struck by a club with little loft or by a club whose loft has been to some extent neutralized by the stance, the address, and the action of the player. It runs a long distance after striking the turf, and the inference is that it has been hit without any suspicion of "jabbing" or "stabbing." This inference, moreover, is strengthened by the fact that the ball travels very evenly and steadily and goes further than it appears to have the power to do. Now, observe carefully the action and stance of the player. His weight is forward on the left leg, the ball is toward his right foot, and consequently his hands, when he addresses the ball, are in front of it. This is exactly the position one would expect after watching the flight and run of the ball. The up-swing is short, slow, and deliberate, and the down-swing is short, slow, and deliberate - the movement is even and delicately controlled from beginning to end. The club-head almost caresses the ball; if it is slow to reach the ball, it is loth to leave it.

It is by drawing attention to these points that Ernest Jones teaches the run-up. Clearly visualize the shot, gain control of the club in the fingers, then play the shot. It is the fact that the right hand turns over to some extent, but that turning over is only an incident in the shot. It is not the essence of the matter. The essence of the matter is a clear conception of the nature of the shot, and that sense of "touch" which can only be obtained by means of finger control. It is quite easy to turn over the right hand without having any real control of the club whatsoever - one has only to observe the game of the average amateur to realize that this is so. The golfer must, if he is to do any good, learn to differentiate between symptoms and causes, and he must always be on the alert against the teacher who directs him to try to reproduce symptoms.

The Pitch, Pitch And Run, Push Shot, Etc

What has been said of the run-up is equally applicable, with the necessary changes, to all the other shots. The player should first closely observe the

THE GOLF SWING

behaviour of the ball, then the attitude and action of the expert as he makes the shot - always correlating the two things, effect and cause. Then, if he has acquired control of the club in his fingers, he will have no difficulty in expressing what he has in his mind. And that is the essence of golf.

3 THE SWING

Fig 24. Quarter shot

Fig 25. Half shot

Fig 26. Full iron shot

THE GOLF SWING

Fig 45. Shows "give" of fingers in any flexible movement

3 THE SWING

Fig 46. Figs 46 and 47 exemplify again the essential "give" of the fingers

THE GOLF SWING

Fig 27. Corollary to fig 24

3 THE SWING

Fig 28. Corollary to fig 25

Fig 29. Corollary to fig 26

THE GOLF SWING

Fig 32. Perfect finish of short iron shot. Contrast with figs 30 and 31, and note how the club-head has been forced through

3 THE SWING

Fig 33. How the blade of the iron should normally come onto the ball

Fig 34. Another view of the type of shot shown in fig 32

THE GOLF SWING

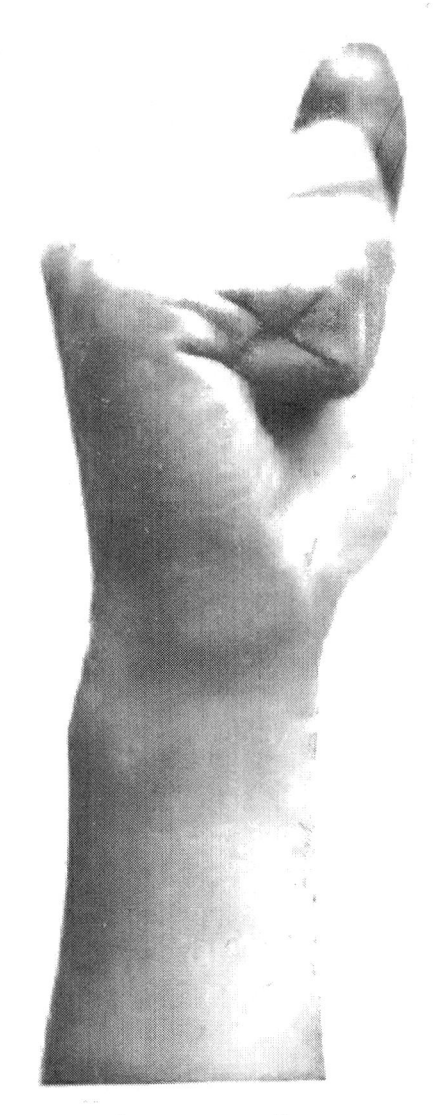

Fig 35. Straight position of wrist

3 THE SWING

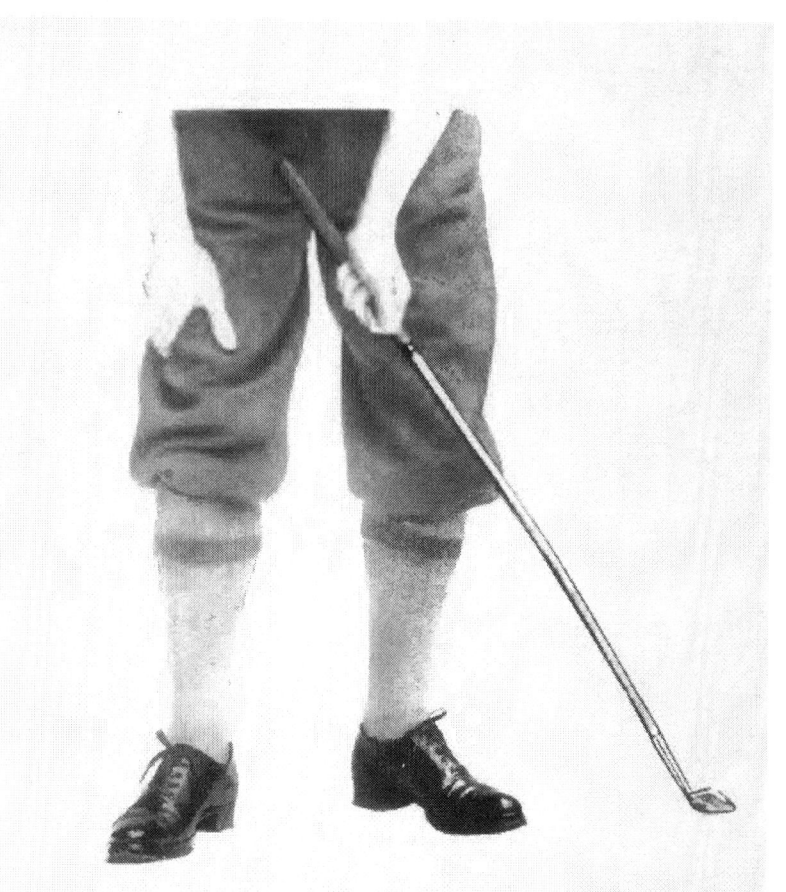

Fig 44. Left wrist bending in follow through

THE GOLF SWING

3 THE SWING

4 THE ACTION OF THE WRIST

I

"I draw it (the club) back close to the ground with my wrists. ... I turn the face away from the ball with my wrists. This turning of the wrists[*] imparts greater speed to the club-head, and is the great secret of long driving. To master this turn of the wrists is to add many yards to the long game. ... After my arms have been allowed to follow through a reasonable distance I turn my wrists and finish the stroke over the left shoulder." - Jerome D. Travers.

* * *

"Now we have seen the operation as it should be - the inward turn of the left wrist. . . .

The left wrist has not turned sufficiently."- Vardon.

* * *

"The first movement must come from the wrists. They and they alone start the head of the club moving back from the ball.

"The initiative in bringing down the club is taken by the left wrist. ... At this point - about a couple of feet from the ball - there should be some

---

[*] Any "turning" is, or course, a turning of the forearm, not of the wrists.

THE GOLF SWING

tightening up of the wrists. . . . I am certainly one of those who believe that the work done by the wrists at this point has a lot to do with the making of the drive. . . ."- Braid.

* * *

"The movement of the upward swing must be begun entirely with the wrists . . . the majority of beginners, instead of letting their wrists do the work ... It is the left wrist begins the downward swing. ... At that moment (when the head of the club is separated from the ball by a space of twenty inches or thereabouts) the two wrists come into play." - Arnaud Massy.

* * *

"Bring it (the club-head) behind the ball with a fairly flat swing, and give it a little flick with the wrists so as to introduce plenty of vim.

"When the club is about eighteen inches from the ball I hit with the back of the left hand, and at the same time put in that right wrist flick which counts for so much." - Herd.

* * *

"The most notable changes with regard to the swing are . . . the wrists come much more into the stroke, the body much less. . . . We note the strong flexion* of the wrists. ... It is very nice to be able to drive a ball two hundred yards with this power of fingers and this turning of the wrists. . . . Taylor, though he uses his wrists freely, has not the Vardon flex or flick, but he gets there just as well with his forearm work. . . ." - John L. Low.

* * *

"The left wrist takes the club back ... If the left wrist is not turned as it should be . . . This turn of the left wrist is a gradual movement. The club-head should meet the ball, the wrists having, in bringing the club down, accelerated the speed at the moment of contact. ... If control of the club is not lost, leverage from the wrists is so much more easily acquired." - J. H. Taylor.

---

* Here used in its popular sense.

4 THE ACTION OF THE WRIST

II

"The object of this book is to show that the mechanism of the golf swing depends on forearm rather than wrist action. Indeed, apart from putting, it will be contended that there is no such thing as a pure wrist shot in the whole domain of golf.

* * *

"The exposition, as well as the performance, of the golf swing is a comparatively simple matter, provided the action of the wrist-joints can be excluded from the movement.

"The wrist-joint, so far from coming into play, is passively rotated backwards and forwards *en bloc* with the hand and forearms.

* * *

"The pace and power of the club-head at the moment of impact are greatly increased by the incipient pronation of the right handwhich contributes the whip-like snap to the movement . . . it is a pure forearm action which takes command of the wrist and hand together.

* * *

"At the moment of impact the sudden tightening up of the muscles of the forearm brings the right hand and forearm from the position of slight supination to the position midway between pronation and supination; and this movement, in conjunction with the straightening out and extension of the right elbow, imparts the characteristic flick to the club-head.', - Burnham Hare *in "The Golfing Swing."*

III

"First and foremost, and one might almost say simply and solely, there is in proper manipulation the *feeling* that one is hitting the ball by means of the wrists.

THE GOLF SWING

"Take thought only of smiting the ball as with the wrist, and the proper twist or roll, the turn of the right hand over the left at the impact, follows automatically.

"Let everything be contributory to what is *called* and *felt* to be wrist action . . . *forearm action though it be in reality*.

"Let the gentle reader be warned against any conscious effort to twist or roll his forearms.

"It is very hard* for the average man to believe that the feeling of wrist action which produces forearm action is a central feature of good golf action." - R. S. Weir, *Golf Illustrated*, March, 1918.

IV

It will thus be seen that according to Messrs. Braid, Taylor, Vardon, Travers, and Low, and, indeed, ninety-nine first-class golfers out of a hundred, the essence of the shot is to get the wrists into it; that according to "Burnham Hare" (who may be taken as fairly representing the anatomical school) the essence of the shot is to keep the wrists out of it; and that according to Mr. R. S. Weir, an engaging exponent of the humanistic compromise, the essence of the shot is to get the forearms into it by aiming at getting the wrists into it. In a word, Messrs. Braid and Co. say the action is a wrist action, so work the wrists; Messrs. Hare and Co. say the action is a forearm action, so work anything but the wrists; while Messrs. Weir and Co. say the action is a forearm action, so work the wrists.

V

Messrs. Weir and Co. appear to proceed on ' two reasonable hypotheses. The first is that it is almost inconceivable that such accomplished players as Messrs. Braid and Co. can be wrong in their *feeling* for the shot. The second is that it is almost inconceivable that such erudite anatomists as Messrs. Hare and Co. can be wrong in their analysis of the shot. What, then, is the explanation of these seemingly contradictory propositions? If A is right in what he says, and B is right in what he does, B must, all unconsciously,

---

*   Quite so. It is very hard, because the feeling which should be the central feature of good golf action is not wrist action, but hand and finger action.

4 THE ACTION OF THE WRIST

achieve what A says; and may not B's method be the best practical way of producing the effect noted and defined by A? After all, the only thing B really has in view is to hit a good shot. After making many good shots and many bad ones, he becomes conscious of certain differences of feeling as between the good shots and the bad ones. It seems to him that when he is hitting good shots he is using his wrists freely, and that when he is hitting bad shots he is failing to use his wrists freely. That is enough for B. And nothing that A can demonstrate will affect him.

But there is C to consider. Is C to follow B and think of his wrists, whilst admitting that the essential action is forearm action as stated by A? Or can C be given some surer guide to success? Is it certain that Messrs. Hare and Co. are entirely correct in their theory that the action is purely forearm action? Or may it be that the wrist-joint plays a real part in the movement? In other words, may there be something in the wrist theory even from the anatomical point of view?

In order to answer this question, one must first determine whether the much-discussed action of the wrist is entirely forearm action, entirely wrist action, or both forearm and wrist action; and one must also determine whether the action, whatsoever it may be, is an initiatory or merely a resultant action, whether it is a cause or an effect.

VI

The wrist joint in itself is capable of four different movements, and four only. These are shown in Figs. 36, 37, 39, and 40.

With a view to determining to what extent, if any, these movements take place in the course of the golf swing, the reader is invited to take hold of a club in each hand successively, and then in both hands together, and to make the complete swing, slowly observing the wrists all the time.

He will observe the following points:

Right Hand

THE GOLF SWING

Up-swing: (a) The wrist-joint moves as shown in Fig. 41, and is extended to the full by the time the arm has reached the position shown in Fig. 42 ("extension" is complete*).

(b) The remainder of the upward movement is achieved mainly by the arm, but at the last moment the wrist-joint gives, allowing the hand to incline towards the shoulder (abduction), and at the same time the fingers give.

Down-swing: The movements involved in the up-swing are reversed.

Follow-through: There is no movement of the right wrist-joint after the club-head has passed the ball, except for the almost negligible abduction of that joint at the end of the swing; what happens is that the forearm turns

Left Hand

Up-swing and down-swing: There is no movement of the wrist-joint except for the almost negligible abduction of that joint. The forearm turns (Fig. 21).

Follow-through: The wrist-joint bends, as shown in Fig. 44.

Both Hands

To recapitulate (ignoring for practical purposes the feeble movements called abduction and adduction):

1. ***From Address to Impact:*** First part of upswing and last part of down-swing: a vigorous movement of the right wrist-joint ("extension"); no movement of the left wrist-joint, but a turning movement of left hand and forearm.*

---

* This movement is accompanied by a slight responsive turning of the forearm.

* The beginner often finds difficulty in moving his hands in the correct manner at the beginning of the upswing. He is prone either to bend outward the left wrist-joint (flexion), as in Fig. 19, or to go to the opposite extreme and overturn the left hand, as in Fig. 20, loosely known as overturning the wrist. He can, however, always arrive at the proper movement of the hands by noting the position which the left hand will automatically take if it is allowed to accommodate itself to the extension of the right wrist-joint (see Fig. 21). He should not, of course, allow his left hand to be passive when he is making the up-swing of

4 THE ACTION OF THE WRIST

2. ***From Impact to Finish.*** - First part of follow-through: a vigorous movement of the left wrist-joint ("extension"); no movement of the right wrist-joint, but a turning movement of the right hand and forearm.

3. The movement technically called flexion (Fig. 19) does not take place at any part of the swing.

VII

In these circumstances the writer puts forward the following propositions:

1. The expression "the turning of the wrists' (*vide* Messrs. Braid and Co.) is misleading. In so far as the wrist turns, it turns *en bloc* with the forearm, as maintained by Messrs. Hare and Co.; the movement is really a hand and forearm movement.

2. Though the "turning of the wrists "is a misleading expression, the wrist-joints do play a vital part in the swing, Messrs. Hare and Co. notwithstanding; and when Braid says, "the first movement must come from the wrists," he is not so far from the truth as Mr. Hare suggests. At all events, an essential and a pronounced part of that movement does come from the extension of the *right* wrist-joint.

3. As regards the whip-like snap which occurs at the moment of impact in a well-hit shot, the popular view that the snap is produced by a "wrist flick," though not quite correct, is preferable to Mr. Hare's "incipient pronation of the right hand."

4. Mr. Hare's statement that the movement is "a pure forearm action which takes command of the wrist and hand together" is unsound in theory, and full of trouble if followed in practice.

5. Mr. Weir concedes too much to Messrs. Hare and Co. as theorists, and too much to Messrs. Braid and Co. as practical teachers. It has been shown that the right wrist-joint before impact, and the left wrist-joint after impact, do play a most important part in the movement, quite distinct from the

---

an actual shot; the left hand should be at least as active as the right, but the complete extension of the right wrist-joint will always give the true position of both hands and arms, and consequently the true course of the club-head.

THE GOLF SWING

turning or twisting of the forearm. But it is to be noted that this movement of the wrist-joint should not be produced by executing the movement as a thing in itself. In the golf swing it is not an initiating movement at all; it is a responsive and contributory movement. The golfer holds the club in his hands, largely in his ringers. Everything that he does with his club is done by means of the hands and fingers. The "feel" of the club, and the power to use the club, come to him through the hands and fingers. "Touch" is entirely a matter of hands and fingers. If the hands are used without finger work, the swing is the clumsy, lumbering movement known as the dead-hand swing. Vitality goes into the swing at the fingers. It is communicated by their controlled extension and contraction (see Figs. 42, 45, 46, and 47). The wrist is a remoter and duller part of the mechanism than even the dead-hand. The player may bring the most practised concentration to bear on the working of the wrists without ever realizing what finger action means, and the fact that, in spite of this concentration on the wrists, many players are so apt at hitting a ball that they also develop perfect finger action is not a good argument for concentrating on the wrists. The average player will doubtless suffer less if he thinks of his wrists than if he thinks of his forearms or his biceps, or his shoulders, or his hips, or his feet; but in nine cases out of ten he will suffer; for though he is nearer to the truth than he might be, he is further from it than he need be. If the rules of golf made it necessary to strap the club to the wrists and not to hold it in the hands, it would doubtless be a good plan to think of using the wrists. But as the golfer does as a fact take hold of the club in his hands and fingers, the writer cannot for the life of him see why he should not try to hit with them.

4 THE ACTION OF THE WRIST

Figs 36 and 37. Two movements of the wrist joint

THE GOLF SWING

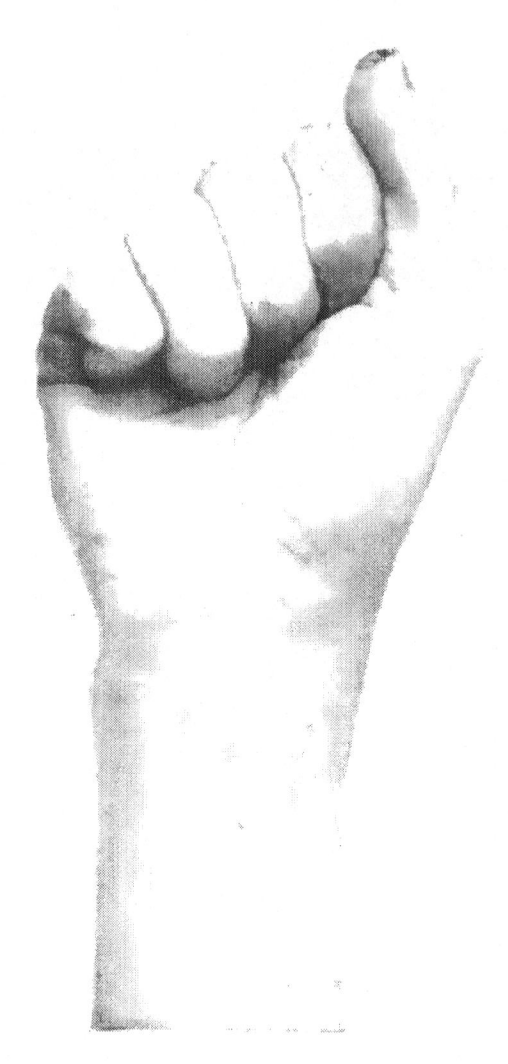

Fig 38. Straight position

4 THE ACTION OF THE WRIST

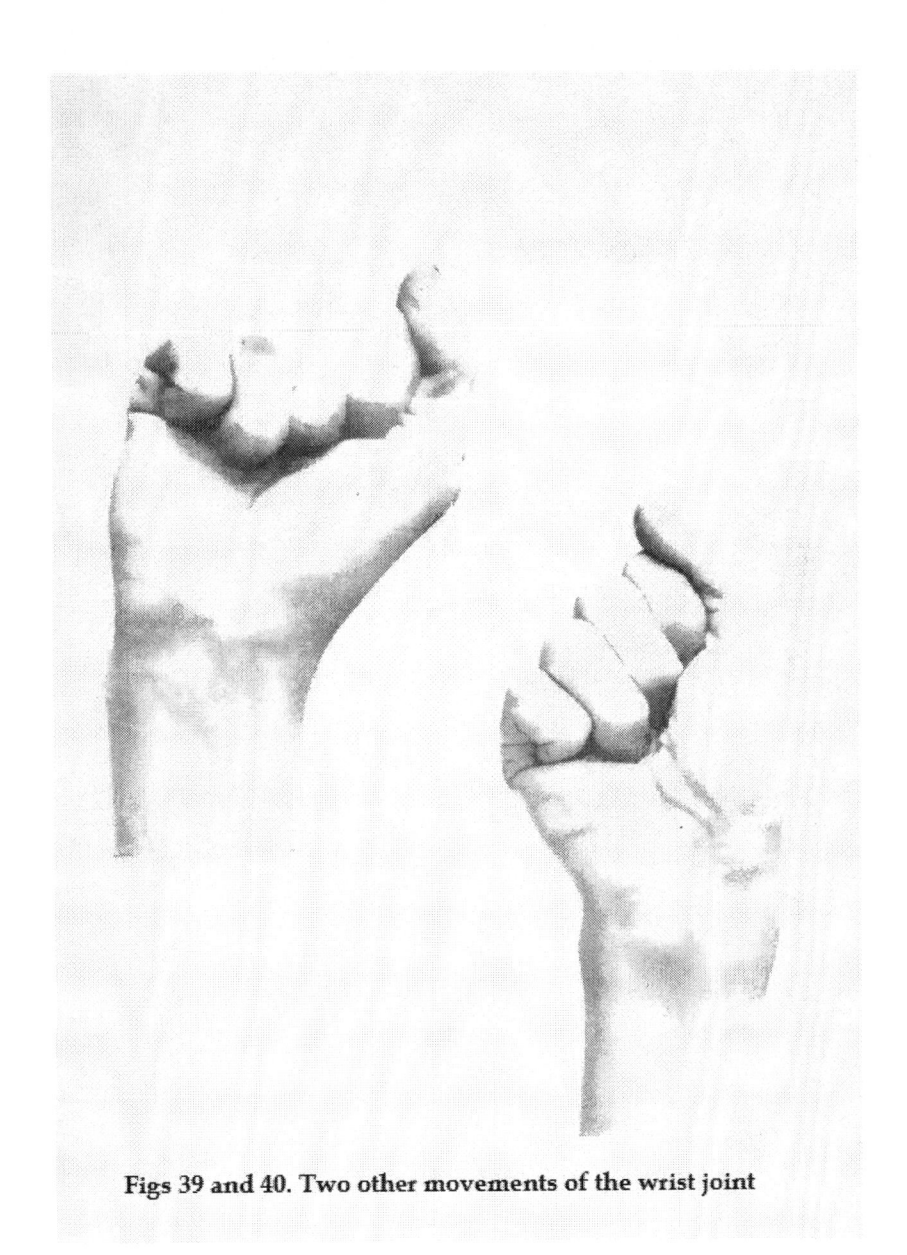

Figs 39 and 40. Two other movements of the wrist joint

THE GOLF SWING

Fig 41. Action of right wrist beginning up-swing

4 THE ACTION OF THE WRIST

Fig 42. The right wrist has been bent as far as it will go

Fig 43. Straight position of right wrist in follow through

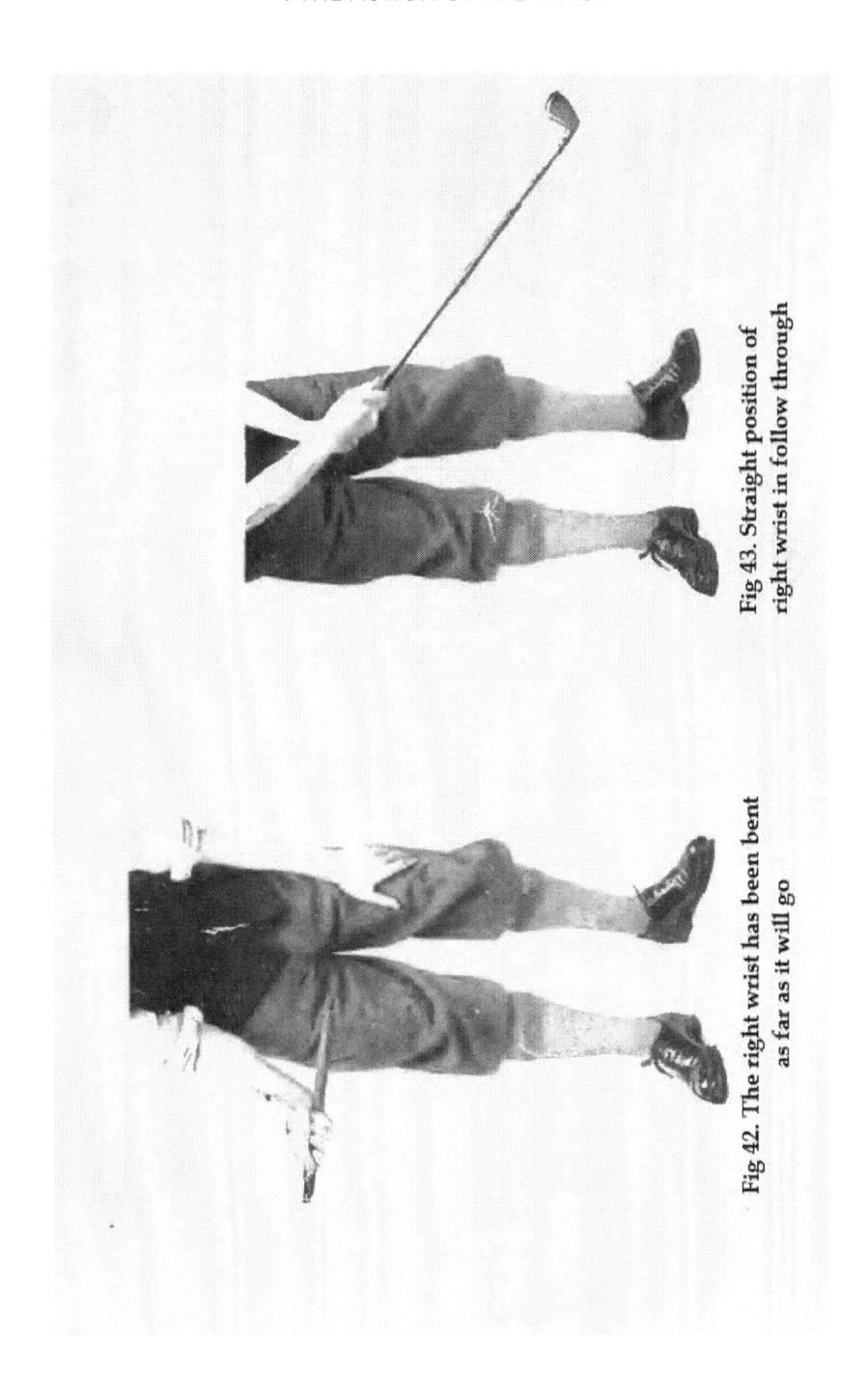

THE GOLF SWING

Fig 47. Compare with fig 46 where the fingers have not "given"

5 THE BALANCE OF THE BODY

In the composition of the golfer the two elements, balance of body and balance of mind are intimately correlated, and from observation one would conclude that neither is easy to maintain. To some extent each may be either a cause or an effect of the other, and whilst it is possible for the one to exist without the other, the two are usually found together - either present or absent.

It is for the reader himself (or herself) to determine whether, and, if so, to what extent, his (or her) faulty balance of body is the cause or the effect of his (or her) faulty balance of mind, and whether treatment should be applied to the one element or to the other, or to both elements.

The writer will not treat specifically of the balance of the mind; for on this point he is ready to receive rather than to give advice; but he will treat specifically of the balance of the body, and it will be agreed that any improvement in the balance of the golfer's body is likely to yield an improvement in the balance of his mind, as a natural consequence.

The type of golfer who regards golf as a game that can be played by anybody, anyhow, finds satisfaction in pointing to differences in the method and style of first-class players. It is not, however, the differences, but the samenesses, that are of real significance. Broadly speaking, indeed, all first-class golfers swing alike. The differences are differences of detail - tricks of personality; the samenesses are fundamental.

THE GOLF SWING

Not the least important of the samenesses is the perfection of body balance, the quality of the even keel. And, conversely, not the least important of the samenesses in the action of bad golfers is the absence of that quality.

The average golfer does not appear to realize the close relationship which exists between the general method of swinging the club and the balance of the body. He thinks of the swinging of the club as one thing, and of the balancing of the body as another thing, and he aims at securing balance by setting his feet wide apart and grimly trying to keep them flat on the turf throughout the swing. This, on the face of it, may not seem to be a wholly bad method. If the player keeps flat on both feet, it would appear to follow that he cannot get on to his toes, that he cannot jump, that he cannot fall away from the ball. But the reasoning is false. Anything and everything may happen to the golfer who tries to root himself to earth in this manner - anything and everything but good golf. For balance is not to be achieved by any short cut; and the effort to do anything with the body or the legs or the feet, beyond allowing them to respond to the movement set up by the hands and fingers, is foredoomed to failure.

There may, of course, be some first-class golfer, unknown to the writer, whose feet throughout the swing remain flat on the ground; but if there is, he proves nothing except that genius, or perseverance, or both, can accomplish most things. Subject to this reservation.

all first-class golfers allow the left knee and foot to give in the up-swing, and the right knee and foot to give in the follow-through, and all first-class golfers preserve an even keel. It is true that Sandy Herd and Edward Ray both sway appreciably in making their shots; but a certain amount of sway is not incompatible with a sustained balance of the body. Both Herd and Ray visualize a certain path for the club-head which the club-head could not follow unless the body were allowed to move outward to the right; but in both cases this movement of the body is just as much a response to the movement set up by the hand and fingers as is the movement of the body in the case of the most perfect corkscrew twister. There is no golfer who conveys more emphatically than Ray the idea that the mastery of the club remains in the player's hands and fingers. At the same time, the writer does not agree with Ray when he says that his sway is the crowning ornament of a finished golfer's style. Fine golfer as Ray is, the writer always feels that he would have been a stroke or two a round still better had he not made his golf

5 THE BALANCE OF THE BODY

a slightly more difficult, a slightly more uncertain, game than even golf need be.

In the orthodox swing the hands and fingers initiate the action of winding the club-head round the body. When the club-head has been got under way a certain tension is felt in the body and legs, and unless this tension is relieved by the giving of the left knee and the left foot, the fingers will cease to control the club-head, the stiffness of the knee-joint will set up an obstacle to their proper functioning, and the balance of the body will be lost. Similarly, if the left knee gives before it receives impetus from the movement set up by the fingers, the mechanism will be put out of joint, and the balance of the body will again be lost.

In the orthodox up-swing, the hips and shoulders must turn so that the left shoulder comes underneath the chin. How can anyone who is not an elastic man or a music-hall artist get into that position unless he allows a certain amount of pivoting to take place? Could this turning movement possibly be made more difficult than by resolutely endeavouring to keep the left foot flat and firm? It is quite clear that something must go - either the ribs or the spinal column, or the balance. Fortunately from the point of view of the death-roll, unfortunately from the point of view of golf, it is the balance that goes in most cases.

The writer had a dear friend whose golfing life had been one long effort to acquire what it pleased him to call a firm stance; but he could be guaranteed to lose his balance every time he essayed anything beyond a quarter-swing. Just before the war broke out he announced confidentially that he had discovered that the secret of a good balance was to plant the right foot firmly on the ground and then to stiffen the right leg so as to form a buttress which should support the whole body. He made an effort to put this great idea into practice, the buttress proved unequal to the strain, and the result was that there was one more cripple in this country and one less soldier than there would otherwise have been. (The number of *golfers* was not, however, affected.)

It is true that in most treatises on golf the golfer is admonished to stand firm on his heels when he is addressing the ball; but in the writer's opinion that advice, having regard to the interpretation normally placed upon it, is bad. In the address the golfer should stand firm, not on his heels, but on his feet. It is with the ball of the foot and the big-toe, as well as the heel, that the good golfer feels himself gripping the turf. Any tendency to get the weight chiefly on to the toes must, of course, be checked; but it should not be checked by going to the opposite extreme of keeping as much weight as possible on the heels. The pedagogy of golf is full of the pernicious plan of endeavouring to get rid of one fault by substituting another fault for it, and the golfer should ever be on his guard against it. To give the feet and legs liberty to move at the dictation of the fingers, is not to invite them to dance a tango or to pirouette in airy independence of the action of fingers, hands, and arms. There is a *via media* between an uncompromising rigidity and a fatuous freedom.

A certain type of golfer habitually keeps an even keel till somewhere about the moment of impact of club-head and ball. At that moment he appears to explode, and the onlooker is surprised that a straight ball of good length is often the result. The explanation of this phenomenon of the links appears to be this: the player regards his duty as done when the ball has been hit - his conception of the golf swing does not take him beyond that point - and he ceases to apply power with the hands and fingers. The result is that the body, which is still under considerable momentum, continues its mad career without the sustained guidance and impetus of its natural leaders, and the swing ends in a sharp sequence of contortions instead of a statuesque repose.

A perfect sense of balance, whether at the top of the up-swing or the finish of the downswing, is only to be acquired by the free action of body, legs, and feet moving in response to the assertive action of hands and fingers. It is to be noted, however, that the specific object of continuous action of hands and fingers after the ball has been hit is not to secure a balanced finish, but to get the last fraction of speed out of the club-head; for the player who aims at continuously developing speed in the club-head after the ball has gone will find it easier to move the club-head at its maximum speed at the moment of impact than he who has no thought of applying power after the ball has gone. The elements in the question are not only mechanical, but psychological.

To resume. The balance of the body is an effect rather than a cause of good swinging; if there is any fault of balance the cause is likely to be found in some fault of swinging (at some point or points in the swing, either the hands and fingers have been lazy, or the legs and body have interfered and not co-operated with them), and the cure is to be found in perfecting the swing.

5 THE BALANCE OF THE BODY

It may usefully be borne in mind that Ernest Jones, on coming out of a military hospital with one leg, played a round of golf, and found himself still on the one leg after every shot he played. One leg, then, is sufficient for balancing purpose if the swing is sound, yet one knows long handicap men who find two legs wholly inadequate for the purpose, and who must surely envy the centipede.

The sure guide to the feet is the fingers.

THE GOLF SWING

Fig 48. An ideally balanced position at the top of the up-swing

5 THE BALANCE OF THE BODY

Miss Cecil Leitch

Fig 49. An ideally balanced position at the finish of the shot

THE GOLF SWING

5 THE BALANCE OF THE BODY

THE GOLF SWING

6 STANCE

The text-books on golf all devote considerable space to the subject of stance. Most of them give a dissertation on the rival types of stance, the "square" and the "open," and adjudicate on their merits and defects; they describe the stance which is considered best adapted for each of the various shots of the game; the straight shot, the slice, the pull, the low ball, the high ball, and so on; and they proceed to give measurements whereby, they allege, the correct stance for any shot in particular may be acquired.

The basic principle underlying the bulk of this literature is that the swing is determined by the stance; witness the following dicta:

"*The stance being carefully chosen and analyzed*, all that is left is to hold the club correctly. . . ." - Massy.

" To gain this result . . . *place your left foot* more in line with the ball. . . ." - Massy.

"The swing is, *from the position I have assumed,* naturally a more upright one." - J. H. Taylor.

"[The diagram] may serve a most useful purpose in helping him (the reader) to grasp quickly the principle that *the swing must adjust itself to the stance.* . . . I prefer to stand open, and my swing has, *in consequence,* adjusted itself in the manner described." - J. H. Taylor.

6 THE STANCE

The italicizing is the writer's, but the quotations are taken almost at random, and they fairly represent the doctrine which is to be found, explicit or implicit, in almost everything that is written on the subject - the doctrine that the natural order of events is first stance, then swing; that the stance is a set position consciously taken up by the player in order to produce a certain type of shot. But is this doctrine sound?

After all, what is the player's object when he stands up to the ball? His object is simply to get into that position which will best give him (a) the direction he requires, and (6) the distance he requires.

As regards direction, it is axiomatic that the ball will follow the direction in which the club-head is moving as it meets and "goes through" the ball. The player's position, then, must be such that when he makes his normal swing the club-head will meet the ball and "go through" it in the line of intended direction.

How is the player to arrive at that position? Should he take up his stance by placing his teet and shoulders, according to some method of measurement, in a certain relationship with the ball, and then make his swing, or should he allow his stance to adjust itself to the swing?

According to the authorities, he should adopt the former course; witness the following quotations, which are typical:

"The true position the ball should occupy relatively to the feet, or, in other words, that which the feet should occupy in relation to the ball, is that in which the ball lies on an imaginary line drawn six or seven inches or so to the right of the left heel. . . . The toes should be turned slightly outwards." - Massy.

"If you look at the photograph . . . you will observe that the toe of the left foot is on line b, that is level with the ball, while the right foot is (say) twenty-five inches from the same line, whereas in an ordinary shot it is only nineteen inches." - Massy.

"Refer to the diagram, and you will observe that the ball should lie exactly between your feet, each of which is at twelve inches from the line b, and

THE GOLF SWING

something less than an inch nearer the ball than in the ordinary drive." - Massy.

"The right foot should be moved in a parallel direction with the line of flight until it is just touching the next white line. In other words, the foot should be just over six inches behind the ball." - J. H. Taylor.

"Place the feet so that the ball is in a line about six inches to the right of the left heel." - Braid.

The reader is asked to consider whether this sort of thing seems right; whether, on the face of it, it is likely that the fine, free, slashing movement known as the golf swing can be arrived at in this way; whether the professionals who preach this doctrine practise it; whether an analysis of their play suggests that they have anything of the kind in view when they stand up to the ball. . . .

Let the reader now examine the alternative method, the method of deriving stance from swing. It has been seen that the player's position must be such that when he makes his normal swing the club-head will meet and "go through" the ball in the line of desired direction. If he is not to take up a position in the manner laid down by the pundits, how is he to proceed?

It is suggested that he should make trial swings over the ball until he finds the position in which the club-head is moving along the line of desired direction as it passes over the ball. That position is his stance. As he advances in experience he will be able to dispense with the trial swing over the ball; he will be able to make the necessary adjustments of his feet and shoulders as he waggles the club; and in time he will take up the appropriate position instinctively.

What is true, moreover, for the normal straight shot is equally true of the "advanced" shots, the intentional slice and pull, the low ball against the wind, the high ball down wind, and so on. In setting out to make any kind of shot, the first thing to do is to visualize the shot required, and the path which the club-head must take if the shot is to be achieved; the second thing to do is to find the position which allows the club-head to take that path.

If a slice is required, then the golfer knows that as the club-head comes on to the ball it must be crossing the line of direction, that is to say, it must be

6 THE STANCE

coming in toward the player. He must therefore stand so that in making his *ordinary** swing the club-head passes naturally in that direction.

If a pull is required, then the golfer knows that, as the club-head "goes through" the ball, it must be crossing slightly the line of direction in an outward sense - that is, away from the player. He must stand therefore so that in making his *ordinary swing* the club-head passes *naturally* in that direction.

In the case of the low shot against the wind, it is clear that, as the club-head "goes through ' the ball, it must be descending and tending to keep to the turf as long as possible. In swinging the club with that behaviour of the club-head in view, the player will naturally tend to keep his weight forward on his left foot.

In the case of the high shot down wind the mental picture will be the opposite one: the club-head must be tending to rise sharply as it "goes through" the ball, and the players weight will naturally be kept well back on the right foot, in order that the club-head may take that path.

Such, it is submitted, is the proper view of stance in so far as the direction is concerned. It now remains to consider stance in relation to the length of the shot. The text books are again prolific in suggestions for the use of the inch-tape and for the use of the club-shaft as a stance guide. Thus Braid: "As a general rule, the player should stand just so far from the ball that when the face of the club is laid against it, the end of the shaft just reaches to his left knee when the latter has got just a suspicion of a bend in it."

This kind of advice may be well meant, but it is ill-conceived. It is not only bad in itself, it is bad because it suggests an entirely wrong attitude to the shot and the game. There is no spectacle on the links more pathetic than that of the player whose mind is atrophied and whose bones are stiff with this kind of doctrine. Uric acid is not more insidious or more deadly. It is~ one of the pleasures, and part of the pride, of Ernest Jones that his pupils never look as though they had been taught golf. They proceed from cause to effect and stand up to the ball as though they were going to hit it, and to enjoy hitting it - not as though they were doing a medieval penance, or entering a torture-chamber, or bracing themselves for the crack of doom, or performing a religious rite, or setting a theodolite. . . . All that the player has to do is to

---

* The player is not called upon to juggle with the club.

THE GOLF SWING

stand up to the ball so that he can swing freely, forcefully, and accurately - that is really all that can usefully be said about it. Obviously, if he stands beyond a certain distance away from the ball he will lose his balance and, with it, accuracy, and he will stretch out his arms and stiffen his shoulders so that he must lose freedom and power. And, obviously, if he approaches beyond a certain distance towards the ball, his swing will be cramped and ineffective. A few experiments and a little thought will teach him all that can be learned.

The writer passes to the question of the square and the open stance, a question magnilo-quently described by one of golfs journalists as "The Battle of the Stances" - a thing ranking in importance, apparently, with Marathon and the Battle of the Marne.

The impression of the open stance normally conveyed in the textbooks is that the player's body is so turned that a line across the player's shoulders is approximately parallel with a line across his toes - that the player is, in fact, turned more or less toward the hole. Thus Webb: "The player should slightly face the hole." But this is not so. *The difference between the open and the square stances is essentially a difference in the position of the feet, the difference in the position of the shoulders and hips being slight - almost negligible.* The failure to realize these facts leads to endless confusion.

"Slicing," says Braid, "is commonly due to a faulty stance . . . the right foot too far forward." Again: "The most elementary direction for obtaining a sliced ball is to take your stance with your right *foot* advanced." And Vardon: "In playing for the slice, the stance should be open." The books are, indeed, practically unanimous on the point. They speak continually of the feet, and if they refer, directly or indirectly to the shoulders or hips, they usually mislead. They suggest that the open stance and the slicing stance are one and the same thing; they do not point out that it is the forward position of the right *shoulder* that gives slice, and they do not warn the player that in the ordinary open stance - the stance which gives the straight ball equally with the square stance - the right shoulder must be kept back, and in no circumstances allowed to come forward to the extent suggested by the advanced position of the right foot.

If it were the fact that in the open stance the shoulders did follow the line of the feet, then the open stance would properly be called the slicing stance, as the player can readily prove to his own satisfaction. Let him stand up to the ball in the position just indicated and make an experimental swing over the

6 THE STANCE

ball, observing the path of the club-head as the ball is passed. He will find that as the club-head passes over the ball it is swinging, not in the line of intended direction, but across that line. The stance he has taken up is, in fact, the position in which he would have found himself had he stood up to the ball with a view to the club-head crossing the line of direction - that is, with a view to slicing.

The player is now asked to stand up to the ball (without thinking for a moment about the position of his feet) so that when he makes his experimental swing the club-head shall pass over the ball in the line of intended direction. That is to say, he is asked to stand up to the ball as though he were about to make an ordinary straight shot. Let him now notice the position of his feet. They may be set either "open" or "square." If they are open, let them be placed square. If they are square, let them be placed open. It will be found that this operation can be done with only a very slight adjustment of the line of the shoulders or the line of the hips, and that if the experimental swing over the ball is repeated, the course of the club-head will not be changed. The moment, however, that the line of the shoulders or the line of the hips, is materially interfered with, that moment a fresh direction will be determined for the club-head, with corresponding results in the shot.

It will thus be seen that in analyzing a player's stance the essential characteristic to be noted is the line of the shoulders (and the hips), and not the position of the feet; for the position of the feet may be varied, within limits, at the caprice of the player. In the slicing stance the line of the shoulders is turned towards the hole. And, of course, the converse holds good, the line of the shoulders in the pulling stance being turned away from the hole.

The vital point to observe in the stance for the straight shot is that whether the feet be open or square, the right shoulder is well back. It is the position which that shoulder must take if the player sets about finding the stance by reference to his swing. The player who has this mental attitude to the stance will instinctively adopt a position in which his head will be turned slightly away from the line of direction; he will have in mind a type of swing based on a back-handed "swipe" at the ball with the left hand and arm. Observation of any expert golfer, whether he stand open or square, will show that his head in the address is turned away from the line of direction, and if the backward position of the right shoulder is less noticeable, the player will tell you that *the feeling he has is that the right shoulder is back*. This feeling is one of the fundamentals of golf. This does not mean, of course, that the beginner must place his right shoulder back when he is addressing the ball, for the position is an effect, not a cause. His right shoulder will automatically take its proper position if he has a proper mental picture of the shot.

To recapitulate. The writer submits that it is no part of the player's business to think of the shot in terms of stance. To do that is to put the cart before the horse, to confuse effect and cause. The stance is determined absolutely and entirely by the swing. It is the swing, and the swing alone, which conditions the stance. When the player has learned to swing the club, he will have nothing to learn about stance. Until he has learned to swing the club, he can learn nothing about stance. It is for these reasons that the writer believes that the teaching of the text-books is unsound - the more, not the less unsound, because that teaching is aimed at the beginner. It is quite true that a beginner who has not acquired the art ot swinging the club may perform less egregiously if he measures out his stance with the help of his club-shaft and an inch-tape. The player who tries to hit the ball when the club-head is the length of the shaft from the left knee will, *ceteris paribus*, fail less miserably than the man who can only reach the ball by adroitly springing forward at a well-chosen moment in the down-swing; and similarly the chances of hitting the ball are undoubtedly increased when the feet are out of the way. But, after all, even the person who takes up golf should be presumed to have some intelligence, and it is only fair to him to ask him to use it. It is obviously not good for the beginner to get hold of the right end of the club if he gets hold of the wrong end of the stick.

6 THE STANCE

7 OVERSWINGING

It is the custom to speak of any movement which allows the club-shaft in the up-swing to pass appreciably beyond the horizontal position as overswinging. It does not matter how this position is achieved, whether by relaxing the grip or by carrying the club high over the shoulders, or by both processes combined - it is glibly called over-swinging.

Observation shows that the few players who really control the club usually have an up-swing in which the horizontal position is not appreciably passed, and that the many players who fail to control the club usually have an up-swing (or rather an upward movement) in which that position is left far behind; and these coincidences invite the inference that the test of overswinging is to be found in the length of up-swing.

In the days of the gutty ball, however, no golfer worthy of the name was content with an up-swing which failed to give the club-head a close view of the left heel - witness illustration of such famous players as Douglas Rolland and Lady Margaret Scott; and it would be absurd to suggest that this fulness of movement was mere rhetoric - something flowing out of the exuberant egotism of the player rather than the stern necessities involved by the stolidity of the ball and the length of the club. It would also be absurd to suggest that the good player of those days failed in complete control of the club.

It must therefore be admitted that there is no essential incompatibility between complete control of the club and a luxuriantly prolonged upswing,

THE GOLF SWING

and that, inasmuch as controlled swinging can never be over-swinging - the two terms are contradictory - the test of over-swinging is to be found elsewhere than in the length of the up-swing alone.

Lady Margaret Scott threatening her left heel in the up-swing and her right heel in the follow-through, yet controlled her club. Mrs. X., whilst falling far short of the former achievement, falls still further short of the latter. What is the difference between the swing of Lady Margaret Scott and the swing of Mrs. X.? The difference lies in the fact that the swing of Lady Margaret Scott was a swing, and that the swing of Mrs. X. is not a swing at all. One proceeds inevitably to the generalization that the person who can swing a club will never over-swing it, and that what is called over-swinging is simply not swinging at all. The logical conclusion is that the cure for what is called over-swinging is to be found in learning to swing, and not, as is popularly supposed, in shortening the swing.

Though Lady Margaret Scott might choose to allow the club-head to coquet with her heels, she never permitted the club-shaft to toy with her shoulders. On the other hand, no such restraint on the club-shaft is imposed by Mrs. X.

What happens in the "swing" of Mrs. X. is this: (1) Instead of being set in motion by hand and finger work, the club is pulled away from the ball by the premature turning of the shoulders. (2) Instead of being incessantly moved round the body by hand and finger work, the club is lifted more or less vertically upward, and the shoulders having expended their energy too soon, now find themselves without stimulus to further action; they therefore cease to turn. (3) The whole mechanism is by this time out of gear - the movement is obviously incomplete; the player's position is cramped and feeble: she must free herself somehow; but the body is rigid and the arms have gone as far as they will go. Something has to give way - the fingers oblige, the grip is relaxed, the club-shaft strikes the shoulder and rebounds. (And this rebound is the beginning of the down-swing !) Instead of an up-swing, there are three movements - a drag, a lift, and a flop - and the down-swing is inaugurated with a jerk !

Now, what is the attitude of Mrs. X. to her incompetence? As a rule she resigns herself to what she deems to be the inevitable - it is not, she argues, given to everyone to play like a professional, and it is evidently in the nature of things that she should drag, lift, flop, and jerk the club rather than swing it.

7 OVERSWINGING

... But Mrs. X. may be of different texture. She may be determined to rid herself of the scourge at all costs. How does she set about it - in the normal case?

In the first place she makes a wrong diagnosis. She commits the cardinal error of confusing symptom with disease. She regards the flop as the disease; she ignores the drag and the lift which precede it. To her mind the movement goes wrong at the moment she relaxes her grip, and not before. Alternative methods of treatment promptly suggest themselves to her. The first is to maintain at all costs a fiercely tight grip throughout the movement. The second is to stop the movement before the temptation to relax the grip becomes pronounced. The effects of the first method need not be dwelt upon. It is enough to say that golf can never be amongst them. The second method may usefully be analyzed.

What is Mrs. X. left with when she has eliminated the "flop" from the upward movement of her club? Is it anything more nearly resembling a swing than it was before? It is not. She has made no material alteration in her action. She has left the root and the stalk of the weed and merely cut off the flower. Instead of drag, lift, and flop, her action is now drag and lift. That is all. Mrs. X. doubtless regards herself as a short swinger. But she is not. She is merely a caricature of a short swinger. Even the short swinger must be given his due. ...

What, then, is the typical action of the short swinger?

The short swing properly so called is a swing which is quite sound as far as it goes (Fig. 52). It is the ordinary up-swing stopped short of its maturity. It is, in fact, the swing normally adopted for an iron shot. It is the ideal swing for an iron shot because it lends itself to the exact placing of the ball. It is not the ideal swing for a wooden club shot (in ordinary circumstances) because a longer swing will give greater distance and as much accuracy of direction as is normally required in a shot with a wooden club. The question, it will be observed, is, like most other questions, one of compromise. Every shot in the game must have two qualities - a certain length and a certain degree of accuracy. The proportion between these two qualities varies in different shots, and the type of swing varies with it. Normally the full shot with a wooden club is the one in which the element of accuracy is most subordinated to the element of length. But even in this shot only a small degree of variation is

THE GOLF SWING

possible, and the swing must therefore always be thoroughly controlled - whatever its length.

It has been seen that the players of a past generation were able to control a longer swing (see Fig. 50) than the swing now favoured. But experiment will show that the difficulty of control is increased when the swing is lengthened beyond a certain point.

The problem presents itself in this way. The gutty ball is an unresponsive thing compared with the rubber-cored ball. It requires a greater effort to drive it a given distance, but its behaviour on being miss-hit is less erratic. In these circumstances the golfer was preoccupied in getting the utmost length of which he was capable, knowing that if he did not hit the ball quite accurately - so long as he hit it freely - it would not behave in the eccentric manner of the modern rubber-core. In other words, of the two qualities of accuracy and length, he could afford to think more of the latter than the former. He chose, therefore, a club with a long shaft, and adopted - largely as a consequence of using a long-shafted club - a long and exuberant swing.

With the modern ball, however, it is found that no greater distance is obtained by using a long-shafted club and prolonging the up-swing beyond a certain point, whilst accuracy is endangered; and the expert wisely contents himself with an up-swing finishing in the region of the horizontal position. But this up-swing, though short in comparison with the up-swing of twenty years ago, is a complete up-swing. The club is taken back as far as it will go on the basis adopted. The hands and arms have described a spiral round the body and the body has twisted in response, and the club comes to rest at the top of the up-swing, not because the player actively stops it at that point, but because fingers, hands, arms, body, legs and feet have completed their work (Fig. 48). If the club went further, the player would fare worse - he would be a surgical case.

It is of the very essence of the golf swing that the club-head should be kept moving all the time. "Keep the club-head moving ' might well be substituted for "Keep the home fires burning." And the shoulder hitter who thinks to cure himself of his disease by stopping the club at a chosen point in the up-swing is "flying in the face of Providence." He wantonly stops the movement of the club at the very moment when the hands and fingers should be forcing it into a position of precision and power. Let him take his courage as well as the club in both hands, and at the point when he imagines the fatal

7 OVERSWINGING

flop is about to begin, let him force the club-head resolutely further behind his head by persistent hand and ringer action. He will then find that the shaft will not strike his shoulder, and that the up-swing will stop when the hands and fingers have accomplished the fullest natural movement of which they are capable.

Under-swinging is not less of a vice than over-swinging, and the golfer should always be on his guard against it. For under-swinging is neither more nor less than the failure to make full use of the hands and fingers. It is just as easy to under-swing in a short mashie chip as in a full swing; for even in a short mashie chip the hands and fingers should function to the fullest extent possible having regard to the type of the shot.

It is this determination to move the club-head as far as possible with the hands and fingers at every point in the swing which is at the root of all good golf. It precludes the possibility of relaxing the grip, of shoulder-hitting, and other pathetic symptoms of incompetence (see Figs. 51 and 53); and it allows the player to get the utmost speed and the finest precision out of that good servant, but bad master, that faithful friend, but bitter enemy - the club-head.

THE GOLF SWING

Fig 50. The old-fashioned up-swing: exuberant, yet controlled. A slashing and powerful movement.

Fig 51. Clumsiness and lack of control

7 OVERSWINGING

Fig 52. Good as far as it goes

THE GOLF SWING

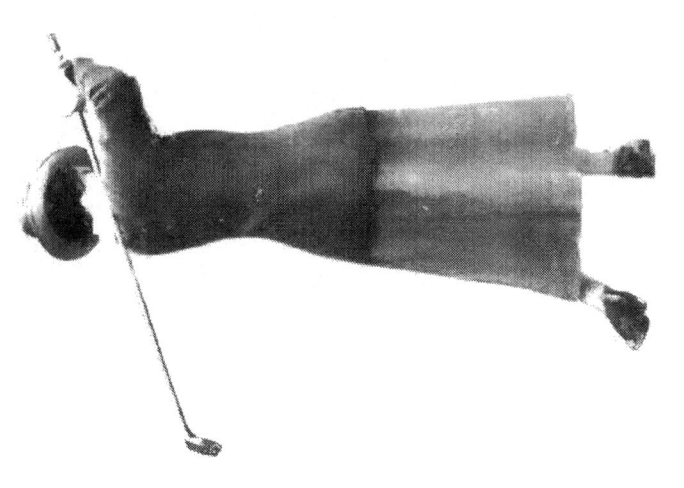

Fig 53. A frequent sight on the links

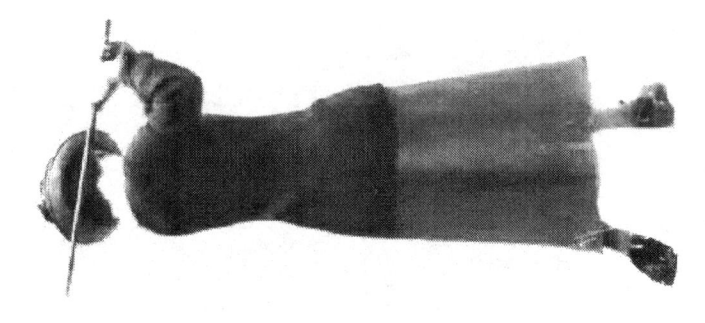

Fig 54. A trifle too careful

7 OVERSWINGING

Fig 55. Compare with fig 50

THE GOLF SWING

THE GOLF SWING

8 SOCKETING

It is one of the many ironies of golf that some of its maladies beset the mature player almost equally with the novice; and of these maladies socketing is perhaps the chief. Not even players of the first flight are immune from it. The writer knows many scratch and plus players whom it victimizes from time to time - occasionally over long periods. One of these is an English international of golf-wide reputation who distinguished himself in an international match by an orgy of socketing, resulting (so far as international matches are concerned) in a record round for the number of holes lost. Another is an open champion who for months failed to hit a mashie shot off the middle of the club-face except by accident. It is, of course, to be expected that the novice should be capable of any golfing enormity - he may give at the knees, he may fall forward whilst trying to hit the ball, he may refuse to work his elbow-joints, he may do a score of things he ought not to do - and socketed shots may be the result of any one of them. For him there is but one method of treatment: he must learn to swing properly; and there is nothing more to be said. But the case of the mature golfer who falls a victim to socketing may be analyzed usefully; for his knowledge of the game is such that he is able to appreciate points which could but befog the beginner.

As first sight it seems that there must be something in socketing which even in golf is unusually mysterious. The writer is, however,, of the opinion that the mysterious element is rather apparent than real, and that the practised eye can always trace the germ of the disease in the normal action of any mature player who is capable of periods of socketing.

8 SOCKETING

The player is recommended to analyze the normal socketed shot on the following lines:

(1) To note the position in which he finds himself, and the position in which he finds the club-head, at the finish of the faulty shot.

(2) To compare these positions with the corresponding positions in the correct movement.

(3) To discover what method he would adopt if he wished to commit the fault he is trying to cure.

(4) To compare this method with the method of attaining the correct positions.

(5) To locate - by means of the comparison

- the point at which the differentiation begins, and to identify the particular action which distinguishes the correct shot from the faulty shot.

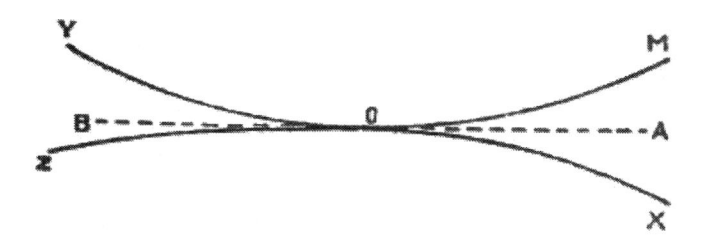

Proceeding on these lines, the writer offers the following observations on the socketed shot:

(1) (a) The player's right shoulder has not followed on in its natural curve; its movement has been checked at some point either before or at the moment of impact. (b) The club-head has finished, not to the left, but to the right of the line of desired direction.

(2) In the diagram, AOB represents the line of desired direction, XOT the path of the club-head, XOZ the path the club-head should have taken.

THE GOLF SWING

(3) Experiment will at once show that in order to make the club-head take the line XOY, the best plan is -

(i.) to keep the right shoulder from turning;

(ii.) to keep the hands and fingers inactive; and

(iii.) to push the club-head out in the line OY by straightening out the right arm at the elbow-joint, and by preventing the right forearm from turning from right to left.

(4) When the club-head takes the proper line XOZ, it is found -

(i.) that the right shoulder responds to the pull of the club-head;

(ii.) that the hands and fingers assert themselves and make the club-head do its work; and

(iii.) that there is no stiffness anywhere, the right forearm turning freely from right to left in response to the impulse set up by the hands and fingers.

(5) The differentiating movement is really performed by the hands and fingers. If these are made to do their work and the body and arms are allowed to move so as to give them free play, the club-head will take, not the line OT, but the line OZ.

The reader will probably have noticed some similarity in the behaviour of the club-head in the socketing shot and the behaviour of the club-head in the cut-mashie shot. Indeed, socketing is often the outcome of playing the cut-mashie shot with stiff forearms.

The cut-mashie shot can, however, be played with safety if two points are borne in mind:

(i.) The directing energy should be determinedly applied through the hands and fingers; and

(ii.) The club-head should travel, not in the line XOY, but in the line MOZ.

8 SOCKETING

[In the up-swing it should travel outside the line of direction, and in the follow-through inside that line, whereas in the socketing movement it travels, in the up-swing, inside the line of direction, and, in the follow-through, outside that line.]

The push-shot (Fig. 58), even more than the cut-mashie shot, bears certain outward resemblances, and oftener than not, alas ! certain inward resemblances, to the socketed shot (Fig. 56).

In the push-shot there is, of course, considerable firmness of wrist and forearm; the clubhead follows through further on the line of flight than in the ordinary iron shot; and the toe of the club does not get in front of the heel. The margin of error is obviously small. If instead of taking the line XOZ, the club-head goes outward ever so slightly in the line XOYy the shot will be socketed.

Nearly all the textbooks and nearly all the teachers make a fetish of the essential difference between the iron shot (ordinary as well as push) and the swing with the wooden clubs. The player is told that in playing his irons the grip must be firmer, the arms and wrists tauter, the body more rigid, the up-swing shorter, and so on.

The effect of this teaching is to stiffen and cramp the iron play, even of many first-class players: in a word, to implant in it the seed ot socketing, a disease which, it is vital to note, is practically confined to play with iron clubs and has no counterpart in wooden club play. There is no essential difference in the manipulation ot iron and wooden clubs, and socketing would be rarer if this fact were recognized and iron shots were made with some of the freedom which distinguishes wooden-club play. The golfer must gain control of the club - whether iron or wood - in his hands and fingers. He must know clearly the manner of the flight of the ball that inevitably results from a certain type of swing, and he must make the club-head perform the desired type of swing by means of appropriate hand and finger action. If he wants to force an iron shot against the wind, he will obviously not flick the ball lightly into the air with a delicate movement of the fingers; he will beat it down and forward by actions at once definite and powerful. But those definite and powerful actions should be the result of hand and finger work consciously applied. They should not be the result - as is so persistently urged by those who mistake symptoms for causes - of holding the body, the forearms, and the wrists rigid or of gripping the club with vice-like pressure.

If the seat of control is in the hands and fingers, the player can produce any one type of shot as readily as any other type of shot. It is just as easy for him to make the club-head finish in front of him, as in the push-shot, as to swing it heroically over his left shoulder. If the club-head stops in front of him he will notice that the forearms and wrists are taut. He has, in fact, produced the shot in such a manner that the wrists and forearms must be taut. This is a totally different matter from trying to produce the shot by means of taut wrists and forearms. The difference is the difference between cause and effect. Thus in the case of the push-shot, if the player aims at producing the shot in the correct manner - that is, by a movement of the club-head dominated by the fingers - he will never be likely to socket. If, however, he aims at producing the shot by stiffening certain limbs and muscles, he will never - despite any success he may achieve - be an entirely sound golfer; he will always be more or less liable to lapses from form, and amongst the lapses socketing will most probably find a place.

The following propositions are offered for the reader's consideration:

The player can never socket who keeps control of the club in his hands and fingers and does not interfere with the responsive movements.

Socketing may occur whenever the stiffening of the arms or wrists or body interferes with the full and free working out of the swing at the instance of the hands and fingers.

The time-honoured doctrine of accentuating the follow-through along the line of flight or throwing the arms out after the ball, is a dangerous one; it tends to devitalize hand and finger work, to stiffen the forearms, and to put the line of the follow-through out of true relation to the line of the up-swing.

The caddy's advice to stand further away from the ball is pernicious; if carried out, it is likely to accentuate the stiffness which is the cause of the disease.

The advice of the club-seller to buy a set of non-socketing irons should be ignored even by millionaires. Non-socketing irons have one grave defect: they socket.

8 SOCKETING

The advice to keep the right elbow close to the side, the right arm close to the body, and the left elbow close to the side, is not good; these positions are symptoms, not causes, of properly hit shots; and if the player concentrates on making his swing conform with a number of fixed points instead of so producing the swing that it must conform with those fixed points, he will inevitably deaden it. The true golf-swing is to be achieved, not by *placing* the body and the limbs into a series of carefully chosen positions, but by learning how to communicate life to the club-head through the fingers. The artist gives life to his line, not by tracing the line through a series of points, but by making one unfettered sweep of the pencil - he communicates life to the line through the fingers. . . .

The socketer will appreciate that alternatives are open to him: one is to learn to swing properly; the other is to give up the game. The writer apprehends that the former course will normally be followed as being the easier of the two.

Fig 56. The socketing position *par axcellence*

8 SOCKETING

Fig 57. An ideal finish

THE GOLF SWING

Fig 58. The push shot

8 SOCKETING

Fig 59. Note the delicacy and freedom of the finish of this iron shot

Fig 60. The finish of a firm iron shot

8 SOCKETING

Mrs. Alan Macbeth
(Miss Muriel Dodd)

Figs 61 and 62. Two perfect iron shots. Note the essential similarity of the positions. No suspicion of stiffness or rigidity.

THE GOLF SWING

Fig 63. Finis.

8 SOCKETING

THE GOLF SWING

9 SOME OTHER ENORMETIES

Sclaffing and digging

Sclaffing and digging differ from most faults in that the player is conscious of them before the ball is hit away. In both cases the club-head meets the ground before it reaches the ball; but though the two faults have this point in common, they are essentially different. In the sclaffed shot the club-head passes more or less lightly along the turf, the rhythm of the shot is not necessarily lost, and the speed of the club-head may not be seriously reduced. But in the shot known as digging, the club-head digs into the turf, the rhythm of the shot - if it ever had rhythm - is inevitably destroyed, and the movement of the club-head is piteously retarded. Sclaffing is by no means synonymous with foozling; digging is one of the most common forms of foozling.

An analysis of digging will show that in the down-swing the right side of the body has been relaxed, and that the right shoulder and probably the right knee have dropped. In short, the hands and fingers have failed to assert themselves, and the action has been led by the body. The player has really been trying to help the club-head on to the ball with his shoulder, instead of controlling the club-head with the hands and fingers and allowing the body to respond. It will be found that it is difficult to drop the shoulder if the swing is definitely made by means of vigorous hand and finger action; but that the moment that notion is lost sight of, the body will come lumbering in, to the utter ruin of the shot.

9 SOME OTHER ENORMETIES

As regards *sclaffing*, the player will gain insight into the disease by asking himself how he would produce a sclaff if a sclaff were desired. He would stand in such a position that the club-head would reach its lowest point in the down-swing before it reached the ball. That is to say, he would stand a little farther away from the hole than he would normally do. It is clear, then, that a false stance may be responsible for sclaffing. As pointed out in the chapter on faults of stance, the stance should always be determined by the swing; and if the method of arriving at stance is followed, the player can obviously never suffer from the kind of sclaffing that comes from a wrong stance.

Is there any other easy way of sclaffing? If instead of allowing his body to be pulled through after the club-head, the player keeps his body back so that his weight at the end of the swing remains largely on the right foot, he will find sclaffing quite simple. And such sclaffing may permit of quite useful shots being made. For here the hands and wrists are doing their good work, and it is only the body that lags to some extent. The cure for this type of sclaffing is obvious. The player must let his hands work out his salvation by placing himself unreservedly in their hands, so to speak. His body must be like the child - it must not speak till it is spoken to, but when it is spoken to it must answer cheerfully and not grudgingly.

Killing

The player will find this operation easy if he determines to use his right hand for the purpose of turning the club-face over toward the turf as the club-head strikes the ball; and the operation will be facilitated if in making the shot he allows his body to turn prematurely so bringing his weight prematurely forward. The confirmed "killer" should note carefully, in the correct shot, the angle of the face of the club with the ground, as the club comes on to the ball and in the succeeding two or three inches of its journey. He should get this picture clearly defined in his mind, and keep it vividly before him when he is making a shot. His movements will soon learn to paint the same picture.

Toeing

On the face of it, toeing appears to be the very antithesis of socketing, but the two things have much in common. In the chapter on socketing it has been shown that the easiest way to socket is, as the club-head comes on to the ball, to stiffen the elbow-joints and to fail to use the hands and fingers, the effect being that the body, no longer under any impulse to turn, stops, with the shoulders facing the direction of the socketed shot. In the toed shot there is, as a rule, a somewhat similar failure of body action, but the hands at the last moment make a desperate effort to put things right and assert themselves. The club-head duly finishes on the left side of the line to the hole, but, the body being out of position, it is the toe of the club and not the middle of the face that meets the ball. The reader will not find it difficult to "toe" in this manner. He has only to check the natural turning movement of the shoulders and to use his hands at the last moment to find that he can toe nine shots out of ten. If, moreover, he tires of this method, he can achieve the same result by going to the other extreme (how true this is of almost everything in golf!). Instead of arresting the turning of his body, let him encourage it to get always in front of its proper position at every point in the swing, and he will find toeing possible again - not quite so easy as before, but still by no means beyond the average man's powers. Of course, if the player lifts his head as well, the operation will be still further simplified.

Fluffing The Short Approach

There is a strong tendency in making every golf shot to stiffen the wrists and forearms as the club-head comes on to the ball. The tendency is doubtless akin to the tendency to anticipate the kick of the gun in shooting. It takes *' quality" out of any shot and it utterly ruins the short approach, which may be two inches instead of two yards, or two yards instead of twenty. The player should practise these shots with one thing, and one thing only, in view, and that is to make the club-head move "through" the ball by means of persistent hand and finger work unimpeded by any stiffness of wrists or forearms. It will help him in this practice if he will consciously relax all his muscles and his grip except for the first two fingers and the thumb of each hand, and assertively make the club-head travel as far as possible - having regard, of course, to the limitations imposed by the nature of the shot. Let him guard against (i) the tendency to cease to actuate the club-head by means of hand and finger work at some point near to the ball, and (ii) the complementary tendency to stiffen the wrists and forearms at that moment. It is not enough for him to start the club-head down with a certain impetus and then to let it do the work. He must figure out the shot, and work out the shot, on the basis that his hands and fingers are going to keep the club-head moving all the time.

Faults Of Putting

9 SOME OTHER ENORMETIES

These are (a) faults of direction, and (b) faults of strength.

Faults of Direction. - As regards direction, the player has obviously to stand to the ball so that, in making the normal movement of the club, the club-head passes through the ball along the line of direction, with its face at right angles to that line. The stance matters little, provided it is conditioned by the swing.

Faults of Strength. - The writer suggests that the finest control of the putter is likely to be attained by the player who grips mainly between thumbs and forefingers, and persistently keeps the club-head moving by persistent finger work. In this way he gets the utmost out of the club-head within the limits of any particular swing, and acquires a knowledge of what result to expect from the movement he sets out to make. He is better able to judge his effects than the player who checks the club-head and thereby introduces into an alarmingly uncertain thing still one more element of uncertainty. In this respect approach putting has much in common with mashie approaching. (At the same time the writer's advice to those players who can stab long putts up to the hole, and short putts into the hole, is to go on stabbing!)

* * * *

The faults which have been dealt with do not, of course, exhaust the whole tragedy of the game. Golf is not unlike Cleopatra - age cannot wither her, nor custom stale her infinite variety. It is hoped, however, that the suggestions for diagnosis and treatment that have been given are sufficiently broad in principle and sufficiently precise in method to help the victim, no matter what his malady, to make a man of himself, and a golfer.

THE GOLF SWING

10 RECAPITULATORY

GENERAL

THE RESPONSIVE MOVEMENTS

It is one of the misfortunes of golf that the correct playing of the shot should make a pretty picture; the observer - and the player as well - is apt to become too much interested in the pretty picture, that is, in effect, and too little interested in the causes of which that effect is merely an expression. In no other game does the statuesque position occur so regularly. In golf it appears at the finish of almost every properly played shot, from the shortest of short approaches to the longest of long drives. The club, the hands and arms, the shoulders, the legs and feet, are all seen in a more or less stereotyped relationship, all in repose, the repose that is the logical result of well-directed effort, the repose that invites the camera or even the sculptor's chisel. There is nothing comparable with this characteristic in, for example, baseball, football, cricket, tennis, or billiards. In those games the vitally interesting thing is the action by which the result is achieved, not the appearance of the performer when the action is being, or has been, made. And this fact doubtless explains to some extent why in golf the action of the average player looks, and indeed is, so much less spontaneous than in other games.

The footballer kicking a football does not know, or think, or care, where his right knee or his left hip will be at any given moment in the operation of kicking. His mind sends a direction to his feet, and his feet obey if he is a

10 RECAPITULATORY

good footballer, or disobey if he is a bad footballer. The billiard player is not at all concerned with the position in which he will be found at the finish of his stroke. He is not at any moment in the game an inspiring subject for the photographer, much less for the sculptor. He consequently gets on with the work. The mind directs the fingers and the fingers direct the cue. The elbows, arms, shoulders, body and legs also move; they move, however, not on their own account, but in response to the impetus in the cue set up by the action of the fingers. The person performing Indian club exercises never thinks for one moment about the position of his elbows or his knees. What he does think about all the time is the movement of the club, and the action of the hands and fingers by means of which that movement is produced. He is pre-eminently a creature of action, not a hero of repose, and he is not in the least degree interested in what his appearance may be at the **end** of any movement or sequence of movements that he may make.

The footballer's mind is directed to the one point of contact - toe and ball; the Indian club performer's mind is directed to the one point of contact - fingers and club; the billiard player's mind is directed to the two points of contact, cue and ball, fingers and cue. And so the golfer's mind should be directed to the two points of contact, club and ball, hands and club.

The golfer's object is to gain command of a golf club just in the same way as the Indian club performer's object is to gain command of an Indian club. True, it is not necessary for the golfer when making his shot to twist his club about as though it were an Indian club. At the same time, the golfer should be able to twist it about in that manner. He should be able to swing the club about in his hands and fingers, freely and fluently in any direction. The pianist learns all sorts of exercises that never come actually into the performance of any piece of pianoforte music. He does so in order to gain command of his fingers. And in the same way, the golfer will do well to make any and every movement with his club that will increase his skill in manipulating it, increase his sense of intimacy with it, his feeling of power over it. When he is swinging the club about in this casual manner, whether with right hand or left hand, or with both hands, he will observe - if it occurs to him to do so - that though he thinks only of communicating movement to the club by means of his hands and fingers, the forearms, the elbow joints, the shoulders, and probably the legs and feet, are also in action - responsive action; responsive in the sense that they move without any specific direction from the mind, but on the impulse created by the action of the hands and fingers in the club. If an attempt were made to swing the club about by using the hands and fingers to

THE GOLF SWING

the exclusion of the action of other members of the body, that is to say, without the naturally responsive movements, the result would not only be stilted and powerless; it would produce an appreciable strain on the muscles involved.

This is exactly the stilted and powerless movement or series of movements that is known as mistiming the shot. Of the various parts of the body that should act in harmony, some parts act either out of harmony, or not at all. It is good to start the club-head by hand and finger action, but it is useless to do this unless forearms and upper arms and shoulders and hips and legs and feet and head are allowed to follow. Everything must "give" when the call comes - except the grip of the thumb and forefinger of each hand; for with an adequate grip there, control or the club can always be preserved without retarding any responsive movement whatsoever. The responsive movements are just as vital to the proper execution of the shot as the initiatory movements.

One of these responsive movements, as has been suggested, is the movement of the head.

A still tongue may make a wise head, but a still head does not make a wise golfer, no matter what may have been said by the pundits to the contrary. And the pundits have spoken with no uncertain voice. Take a few examples:

Taylor: "[The illustration] shows my head has been kept *immovable* during the back swing, a most important factor in accuracy."

Herd: "Keep that necessary nuisance down as long as you can *as though you had it in a vice*. And keep it down for half a second after you have hit."

Massy: "The player must keep his head *perfectly motionless*."

Vardon is so overwhelmed by the fetish that in his book, "How to Play Golf," he devotes a chapter to it, and recommends the player when practising to tie himself up to a contrivance which tinkles a bell whenever the head moves!

But what is the fact? The fact is that unless the head is allowed to give in the up-swing, in the down-swing, and in the follow-through, the movement

10 RECAPITULATORY

will be cramped and ineffective. So long as a movement is purely a responsive movement it must not be interfered with.

There are, of course, many movements of the head that are not responsive movements, just as there are many movements of the arms and shoulders and hips and legs and feet that are not responsive movements. And all such movements are bad and must be cut out.

To what extent, then, are the movements ot the head in the swing responsive movements? The answer is - to an extent which varies according to the build of the player and his mental picture of the swing.

Take as an example Edward Ray, whose golf is well known on both sides of the Atlantic. Is Ray's head "immovable," "perfectly motionless," rigid as "in a vice"? On the contrary, it moves emphatically from left to right in the up-swing, and from right to left in the down-swing. It would ring Vardon's little bell all the time. Yet Ray is a champion golfer.

It is customary for pseudo-theorists to say that Ray is a genius and can do these odd things; but Ray's view is that his apparently casual attitude to his head is the "crowning ornament" of his style. It is not, however, because Ray is a genius that he can move his head without fatal consequences; nor is that movement the "crowning" ornament of his style. The swing which Ray visualises in his mind is not a swing made about a fixed vertical axis, but a swing made about an axis which is moved sideways thirty or forty degrees by the pull of the club-head. Ray can move his head without fatal consequences because he allows it to move, not on its own account, but in response to an impulse set up by the action of his hands and fingers.

Whilst Ray is an extreme example of head movement, there is probably no first-class golfer whose head does not move in order to allow of a free and full development of the swing. Let the reader try to swing freely whilst keeping his head as rigid as if it were in a vice.

The very idea of the head in a vice is enough to cramp his style.

In these circumstances it will be seen that the cure for head-lifting is not to try to keep the head down till after the ball has been hit away. To try to do that will inevitably destroy the rhythm of the shot and so jerk the head up! The so-called cure must accentuate the disease. That is why players who

THE GOLF SWING

experience a patch of head-lifting are so seldom able to get rid of it at will. The head must be allowed to move responsively - and if it moves responsively it will move evenly. If, then, the player concentrate on hitting the ball he will not look up prematurely. In a word, if he can make the club-head obey his hands, his own head will obey the club-head.

Another golfing fetish is the stiff left arm. The golfer is admonished to see to it that his left arm is kept extended throughout the swing. He is urged to do this consciously. But the extension of the left arm is an effect, not a cause. It is an effect of the proper action of the hands and fingers. When one attempts to catch a ball one does not think of extending the arm; one reaches out with the hands and fingers, and in doing so, one inevitably extends the arm. The extension of the arm is a natural result of the action of the hands and fingers. It is precisely so in the golf swing.

Examples could be multiplied almost indefinitely. The golfer will now be able to find them for himself. And the great lesson for all golfers to learn is this: In the making of the swing two kinds of movements are involved, the initiatory and the responsive movements. For practical purposes the hands and fingers may be regarded as giving the initiatory movements, and the arms, shoulders, legs and feet as contributing the responsive movements. The hands and fingers should be assertive, masterful; the other members of the body ever ready to respond - to speak immediately they are spoken to, but not before.

SOME FURTHER NOTES

METHODS

I.

(i) In the ideal swing the hands and fingers force the pace all the time, and other members of the body and the body itself respond: they do no less; they do no more.

(ii) In the normal shot the club-head, at the moment of going through the ball, is moving on the line of intended direction, and the face of the club is at right angles to that line.

10 RECAPITULATORY

(iii) The player stands to the ball so that in making the swing as in (i) the club-head behaves as in (ii).

(iv) The player keeps his balance; he does this by taking up his position as in (iii), by standing on his feet and not on his heels alone, and by swinging as in (i).

II

When a fault creeps in, or smashes in, to a player's game he should proceed as follows: (a) Reflect that something has gone wrong under one or more of the four heads set out above.

(b) Resist the temptation to move ferociously or gloomily away from the scene of the outrage, and, instead, carefully note his position and the position of the club, so that he may know exactly what sort of caper he has cut.

(c) Compare this position with the relative position in the correct shot, noting the points of dissimilarity.

(d) From the comparison ascertain the method by which the faulty shot can be produced.

III

The player who can most readily produce the faulty shot by design is the player who is least likely either to produce the faulty shot by accident or to be worried by it if he does. To know how to commit is to know how to cure.

PRINCIPLES.

Here are a few of the basic ideas recapitulated. Golf is not a trick, and is not to be learned by trickery. Power is applied by and through the hands and fingers. All golfing faults are aspects of one root fault. Faults occur when the fingers have failed to lead or where the other members of the body have failed to follow. The player should have a clear mental picture of each shot. The player must learn to control the club. The club is a good servant, but a bad master. The body should not be kept back - the hands and fingers should make the club-head lead. There must be no stiffness at any point of the swing. All joints and muscles should be free from tension except those

THE GOLF SWING

concerned in the grip of the forefinger and thumb. Notably, the wrist and forearm and shoulders must be perfectly free. Control in the fingers, and freedom everywhere else - that is the doctrine. The golfer who concentrates on hitting and controlling the ball by the exertion of power through the hands and fingers will not want to look up. Head-lifting is not a disease, it is a symptom of disease: no golfer really impressed with the necessity of controlling the club will be in danger of prematurely lifting his head. The golfer should beware of stiffening the wrist and forearm as the ball is hit - unless it has to be punched out of a bad lie.

The tendency to stiffen the wrist and forearm, and all other evil tendencies, recede when the player concentrates throughout the swing on continuously applying impetus by and through the fingers.

Even though approached from the simplest and the sanest point of view, it is apprehended that golf will still be found to be a sufficiently difficult and elusive game to keep the player's interest alive. Even Ernest Jones nods.

10 RECAPITULATORY

ABOUT ERNEST JONES

Ernest Jones (1887–1965) was an English professional golfer. He is renowned for his accomplishments in teaching many famous professional golfers as well as amateurs. He tutored Virginia Van Wie for many years, including during her stretch of three consecutive U.S. Women's Amateur Championships from 1932–34. He also worked with Glenna Collett Vare, Lawson Little, Betty Hicks, Phil Farley, George Schniter, Horton Smith and other top players of the era.

Early history

Jones was born near Manchester, England. He began playing golf as a young boy and by the age of 18 secured employment at Chislehurst Golf Club as an assistant professional. In 1913 at the age of 25 he was made head professional at that club. As a soldier in the First World War, he was in France. There in March 1915 he was serving in the Sportsman's Battalion of the Royal Fusiliers, near Loos. As the result of an exploding grenade, he suffered the loss of his right leg just below the knee. While a severe injury on its own merit, Jones was afraid it would be a handicap and perhaps be the end to his career as a professional golfer. He was sent back to England where he recuperated for four months. Able to walk using crutches, he proceeded to attempt his first round of golf at Royal Norwich in 1916 where he carded an 83 (38/45) on that first outing. He followed shortly thereafter with a 72 on a long and challenging course. While a relief regarding his prospects for continuing the golf profession, these rounds would prove to bring a surprising and revolutionary change to his concept of golf and its instruction. Later, he was fitted with a prosthetic.

In 1936, at the invitation of Marion Hollins, Jones accepted the position of Head Golf Professional at the Women's National Golf and Tennis Club in Long Island, New York. This was the beginning of a life long career of teaching in the U.S. Subsequent to this position, Jones began teaching in New York city. He had an indoor teaching facility in the Spaulding building at 518 Fifth Avenue.

Instructional development

Jones began to ask himself how it could be that he could yet score so effectively, with such a radical change needing to be made to how his body swung the club having only one leg. Jones himself as well as countless others proved to be able to play well with missing body parts or body parts that were limited in their functioned. Despite the prevalence of golf instruction that described these missing or misfunctioning parts as being essential, Jones and others demonstrated that a golfer's brain would devise compensating strategies to yet produce fine golf shots. This success, in conjunction with his reading of Sir Walter Simpson's book, "The Art of Golf", brought him to the fundamental fact that the key to a successful golf shot was not the correct movement of certain body parts, but the correct movement of the club. Instead of the movement of body parts, the real key was the successful movement of the golf club. Jones had happened upon the then-little-understood fact that the human brain need only experience a persons desire to perform a task. On its own the brain devises a means to create the muscular action to achieve the task. The individual is only aware of "what" they want to do. The brain's action in deciding "how" it will accomplish the task is completely unconscious. This explains how very proficient golfers often report that they have little understanding of "how" they swing and only understand that they can do so when they choose.

Thus it was the case that Jones began his now-famous quest to discover, document, and disseminate a description of "how" the club swung and how to most easily teach the club's movements to others. The result was the writing of many articles on this subject and the publishing of two books. Further, Jones took every opportunity to share his insights with fellow professionals. Jones' simple concept is summarized in this classic "The Golf Swing" instruction. Ironically, it is the drastic simplicity of his approach to golf instruction that met with rancor and objection when he was invited by the PGA (Professional Golfers' Association of America) to present his work. Horton Smith, then the incoming president of the association, told Jones his system was "too simple. We wouldn't sell enough lessons." Perhaps much to the PGA's chagrin, whereas an average pro would have give about 600 lessons a year, Jones would give 3,000. Jones often said, "The trouble with the teaching of golf, is that one is taught what a swing produces [body movement], instead of how to produce a swing [club movement]."

Career overview

His career included playing competitively on the European tour, head golf professional at several of America's most esteemed golf clubs, and a career of teaching both tour professional and amateur golfers. In the years after World War II, he conducted his instruction indoors at the Spaulding Building in New York City. He found that the could achieve better success with his students indoors because they would not be distracted by ball flight and instead focused on performing the swing correctly. Along with Harvey Penick, Tommy Armour, and Percy Boomer, he was inducted into the World Golf Teachers Hall of Fame in 1977.

Made in the USA
Middletown, DE
07 June 2015